Charismata

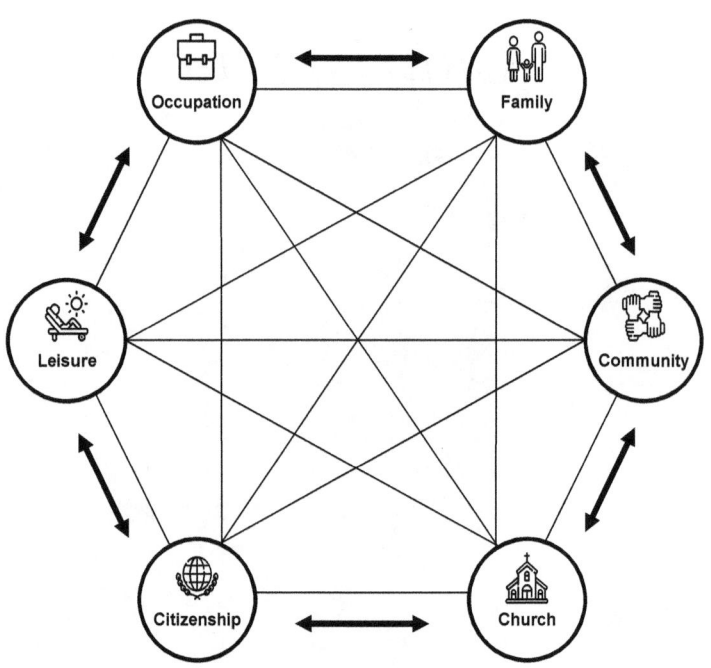

Charismata

A LIFE OF VOCATION

KEN SNODGRASS

WIPF & STOCK · Eugene, Oregon

CHARISMATA
A Life of Vocation

Copyright © 2024 Ken Snodgrass. All rights reserved. Except for brief quotations in critical publications or reviews, no part of this book may be reproduced in any manner without prior written permission from the publisher. Write: Permissions, Wipf and Stock Publishers, 199 W. 8th Ave., Suite 3, Eugene, OR 97401.

Wipf & Stock
An Imprint of Wipf and Stock Publishers
199 W. 8th Ave., Suite 3
Eugene, OR 97401

www.wipfandstock.com

PAPERBACK ISBN: 979-8-3852-1279-8
HARDCOVER ISBN: 979-8-3852-1280-4
EBOOK ISBN: 979-8-3852-1281-1

Unless otherwise stated, Scripture quotations are from the New Revised Standard Version Bible, copyright © 1989 National Council of the Churches of Christ in the United States of America. Used by permission. All rights reserved worldwide.

06/12/24

To Smitty and Tom, who lived significant lives

Contents

Illustrations | viii

Preface | ix

Introduction | xiii

PART I   THE HISTORY OF VOCATION

Premodern (Creation to 1687) | 3

Modern (1687 to 1900) | 53

Postmodern (1900 to Present) | 56

PART II   *CHARISMATA* AND VOCATION

Charismata | 77

Vocation | 101

Appendix: Glossary of Theological Terms | 111

Bibliography | 117

Subject Index | 123

Scripture Index | 129

Illustrations

Figure 1—Theological Model of Work | 77
Figure 2—*Charismata* Portfolio Model | 101

Preface

DURING THE SPRING SEMESTER of 2015, I took the required seminary course *Foundations of Christian Education*, taught by Dr. David F. White, the C. Ellis and Nancy Gribble Nelson professor emeritus of Christian Education. I was not thrilled to take this class because I had no desire to pastor a church. Surprisingly, it was one of my favorite courses. Dr. White emphasized that Christian education is a continual transformation throughout life, not just a biblical introduction for children. After spring recess, we read two books on vocation: Parker Palmer's *Let Your Life Speak* and Brian Mahan's *Forgetting Ourselves on Purpose*. We were required to write two-page reading summaries that covered five topics: problem, solution, appreciation, critique, and application/adaptation. It proved very difficult to condense a book into a two-page, double-spaced paper and cover these five subjects.

I was already mentally formulating the idea of a future book on work and faith. In one of my papers on these vocation-related books, I stated in the application section that I planned to write a book on vocation and would use the materials covered during his course. Upon reading my paper, Dr. White asked me many detailed questions about my book. My initial reaction was: "I had only two pages to cover five topics!" This book, eight years after taking his course, is a more complete response to his questions. Thank you, Dr. White, for opening the world of vocation to me.

I was assisted with the biblical languages by two young and talented scholars. Dr. Robert Jesse Pruett, a graduate in Hebrew studies from the University of Wisconsin, explained the Hebrew

Preface

vocation and gift words and helped me sort them into categories. Dr. Rebecca Moorman, assistant professor in classical studies at Boston University, did the same with the Greek text. Both reviewed the Scripture chapters in their respective fields of study and gave helpful feedback. I have known Rebecca since birth because *Becca* is my niece, who is now a talented woman with a gift for classical languages. She referred me to Jesse for the Hebrew Scripture. Both scholars had to deal with an engineer who created long spreadsheets and asked far too many detailed questions. I am indebted to them for their expertise and patience.

My books contain charts that were designed by Sampath Kumar, managing director and PowerPoint presentation expert at Visual Sculptors Design Services. I have not had the pleasure of meeting Sampath in person because he resides in India. However, his expertise with PowerPoint far exceeded mine. Given our time zone differences, I was able to review his PowerPoint designs when I woke up each morning. The figures and tables are my creations, but it was Sampath who made them clear and understandable.

This book and my first book, *Trading with God*, were impossible to write without my two years of full-time seminary studies at Austin Presbyterian Theological Seminary (APTS). The faculty, administration, students, and alumni created a loving atmosphere of community learning that continued post-graduation. I now serve on the APTS board of trustees, regularly use their outstanding library resources, and seek advice from faculty. The seminary embeds lifelong learning skills that I continue to employ through my writings. I am indebted to APTS and the love they have showered upon me.

I am blessed to have supportive family and friends. My wife, Tracy, read and reread each chapter and provided constructive criticism. My frustration was that I missed so many obvious errors! Theological writings are not her passion, yet she selflessly gave her time. I am so thankful that she is by my side during our bell lap of life together.

This book is dedicated to my parents, Tom and Ida (Smitty) Snodgrass. I won the lottery prize by being born to these two

Preface

Christians. Their love produced four children, six grandchildren, and three great-grandchildren. My parents raised us in the Presbyterian Church and were both active Presbyterian elders. They lived and taught the true meaning of vocation: faith in Jesus Christ and using our God-given gifts in community service. As I grew older, I noticed that my parents grew wiser. Perhaps a little of their wisdom rubbed off on me. They gave me abundant grace during my childhood years when much was needed. My love for them continues to grow as I experience my golden years.

Introduction

> I'm twenty-five, on the shaky
> ladder up, my father's son, Corporate,
> clean-shaven, and I know only what I don't want,
> which is almost everything I have.[1]
>
> STEPHEN DUNN (1939–2021), POET

IN THE LATE 1970S, I was enrolled at the Colorado School of Mines, studying engineering. I was broke and needed to work, but more importantly, I needed time to study. I found employment on campus in the student center, working at the front desk. I strategically worked Sundays from noon until ten p.m. because the cafeteria was closed on Sundays, and few visited the student center during the Denver Bronco football games. My role was to be the eyes and ears in the building while sitting at a desk behind a counter. I studied in this quiet atmosphere and was paid minimum wage.

One Sunday afternoon, a father and his teenage son came into the student center and asked for campus directions. They were touring the campus as a possible school for the son. They asked a few general questions about my school as we informally chatted. I turned to the high school junior and asked, "What engineering major do you want to study?" My university was strictly an engineering school, so the degreed majors were limited.

---

1. Schwehn and Bass, *Leading Lives That Matter*, 438.

INTRODUCTION

His father quickly answered. "My son will study chemical engineering, then work a few years in industry. He will next enroll at a top MBA school. Upon graduation, he will be hired into a fast-track management program and work his way into a senior management position, possibly the CEO."

I turned to the teenager and said, "*So, what do you really want to do?*"

MY JOURNEY

While I have not seen any statistics, I speculate that most people spend more time thinking about *how* to get what they want rather than determining exactly *what* they should want during their life journey.[2] I followed the first approach during much of my life. I wanted to be a corporate manager and engineering seemed the best path. Growing up in south Texas exposed me to the energy business, and my father said, "Engineers run the energy business." I chose chemical engineering because it was easy for me to comprehend chemical processes, and the major offered broad career opportunities.

When I was hired into the upstream side of the energy business, I opted for reservoir engineering for the same reason: it seemed the best route into management. I enrolled in a graduate business school to learn how to manage a business. Once again, my end goal was always to be a manager—the higher, the better. Schoolwork and job assignments, for better or worse, were a means to an end. I just trudged through them. Along the way, I found that I enjoyed the business side of energy far more than the technical. Once I lucked into energy trading, I found my passion in this fast-paced, risky, and highly volatile business. I was not bored with the never-ending, 24/7 trading treadmill, although burnout came during my final years.

The most unexpected and life-changing experience occurred in my mid-thirties when I lived as an expat in London for three

---

2. Bellah et al., *Habits of the Heart*, 21.

INTRODUCTION

years. This period, from 1994 to 1997, transformed my life as I interacted with different cultures and was surrounded by non-Americans. I had to adapt and learn in an environment I did not understand. I was not prepared, and during my first year in London, I made nonfatal mistakes and grew thicker skin from the constant onslaught. I returned to the United States a changed person, mainly for the better. Two more European assignments made me even more worldly. I enjoyed history, religion, literature, and the arts. I traveled widely, both professionally and personally, which continues today. My technological background of black and white shifted into a rainbow of complex colors. I was more human, balancing the technical and economic issues against humanitarian and faith complexities. Two years of seminary study helped further this transformation, although my questions continued to expand.

As I experience the second half of life, I feel more mortal. The earthly journey ahead will be much shorter than the journey to date. I believe that understanding your mortality focuses the mind on life's essentials. To know that you will die is to know how to live.[3] As a teenager and through most of my adult years, I did not dwell on death. My focus was on how to get ahead rather than on how to live a mortal life. This book will focus on how to live.

TRADING WITH GOD: SEVEN STEPS TO INTEGRATE YOUR FAITH INTO YOUR WORK

After seminary, I researched faith and work to answer a vitally important question: *Is the Christian faith relevant in the workplace, and if so, how?* This question was answered in my book *Trading with God*, published in 2019. During my research, I made the decision not to dive deeply into vocation, as the theology of faith and work alone was broad enough to consume one book. Vocation was initially sidestepped and will be addressed in this book.

Vocation and work are not independent. Rather, they are interdependent. As an illustration, vocation is all air traffic, while

---

3. Albom, *Tuesdays with Morrie*, 82–83.

INTRODUCTION

work is regional air traffic. Most people define vocation as a job, occupation, or career. When I was in high school, there was a department named Vocational Training. It comprised learning practical skills like typing or metalworking, rather than book subjects like math, science, and humanities.

Our culture ascribes vocation to exalted professions, such as the clergy, physicians, and first responders. Many of these professions offer relatively less pay for the required training and stress endured, so we elevate a worthy occupation by naming it a *calling*.[4] A few years ago, I asked my church men's group if they felt called to their profession. Going around the table one by one, the doctors, engineers, IT professionals, and others said no. These retired men had just enjoyed doing their work. The last person, a retired minister, said that when he initially went to seminary, he did not feel called to the ministry. But later in his seminary studies he did feel that calling. This book will show that vocation is the comprehensive life of a Christian after positively responding to God's call to faith in Jesus Christ.

THE JOURNEY OF VOCATION

The library is full of vocational books, both secular and spiritual. This book is different from the published literature because it combines scholarly research, which details the journey of vocation from its earliest roots, with practical applications in a vocation model. The book is divided into two major parts.

Part 1 is the journey of vocation. It begins during the premodern period, before the publication of Sir Isaac Newton's *Principia Mathematica* in 1687. The premodern was the prescientific period when cultures had little to no diversity, minimal or no social change, and no secularization. The Old and New Testaments were researched by developing databases of all the Hebrew and Greek verses that contained vocational and gift words. I worked with Dr. Robert Jesse Pruett, at the University of Wisconsin, on

---

4. Wuthnow, *Crisis in the Churches*, 88–89.

INTRODUCTION

the Hebrew text and Dr. Rebecca Moorman, assistant professor of classics at Boston University, on the Greek text. These classical language scholars helped me to sort and categorize biblical texts. The Scripture sections are foundational to understanding vocation. The premodern journey continues through monasticism, the Protestant Reformation, and the English Puritan movement before 1687.

The modern period began with the Age of Enlightenment. This was the beginning of philosophic reasoning and scientific discoveries that questioned religious doctrines and divine revelation. The spirit of capitalism flourished during the modern period in the American colonies under the influence of Calvinism. The early United States Western expansion brought several Christian revivals.

The postmodern period began with the death of Friedrich Nietzsche (1844–1900). Rationality is dismissed, and objective truths do not exist. Moral values are constructed by culture and religious organizations. The journey of vocation continues through early postmodern theologians (Karl Barth, Jacques Ellul) into more recent theologians (Miroslav Volf, Doug Schuurman, and Gary Badcock).

My intention is to help the reader understand how vocation changed from its original Scripture roots into its current, postmodern secular usage. It is only in more recent times that theologians are reverting back to vocation's original biblical meaning and focusing more on using individual God-given gifts in service to the community.

After understanding the vocational journey, part 2 guides the reader through *charismata*, the Greek word for gifts. I will explore individual giftedness, responsibilities within community, and vocational choices. The final section develops a hexagonal *charismata* portfolio model with practical applications for establishing habits and balancing life aspects. This book does not determine the reader's *charismata* nor give a vocational formula that charts their life step by step. It does give guidance, structure, and choices to be made. Only the reader, in freedom, can prayerfully decide on

INTRODUCTION

their individual actions. Only by concentrating on whose we are and what we desire will we live a life of significance.

WHO SHOULD READ THIS BOOK?

This book is meant to help Christians of all ages rediscover the true meaning of vocation, regardless of where you are along the journey of faith. Rather than purchasing a variety of books on vocation that deal with certain aspects of vocation, this book comprehensively traces the journey of vocation and develops applications for use in a postmodern world. The bibliography and cited references can also assist with any further research. A helpful glossary of terms is in the appendix.

This book is also meant for clergy and church workers (teachers, missionaries, and administrators) who need educational resources on vocation and *charismata*, whether for themselves, their church congregations, and/or their larger communities.

BEGINNING PRAYER

All journeys should begin with prayer. My hope is that your vocational journey is as enjoyable as mine was for me.

> My Lord God, I have no idea where I am going. I do not see the road ahead of me. I cannot know for certain where it will end. Nor do I really know myself, and the fact that I think that I am following your will does not mean that I am actually doing so. But I believe that the desire to please you does in fact please you. And I hope I have that desire in all that I am doing. I hope that I will never do anything apart from that desire. And I know that if I do this you will lead me by the right road though I may know nothing about it. Therefore will I trust you always though I may seem to be lost and in the shadow of death. I will not fear, for you are ever with me, and you will never leave me to face my perils alone.[5]

---

5. Thomas Merton, American Trappist monk (1915–68), in Schwehn and Bass, *Leading Lives That Matter*, 450.

PART I

The History of Vocation

Premodern (Creation to 1687)

SCRIPTURE: OLD TESTAMENT

THE STORY OF VOCATION begins with Scripture in the Old Testament (OT),[1] which contains thirty-nine books with 569,174 English words. It begins with a search of the OT verses that contain eight English vocational words (uninflected Hebrew form and derivatives/cognates): anoint, call, choose, invite, made king, separate, set apart, and summon. This word search produces 604 English words and 597 Hebrew words. The differences reflect the translation technique of the New Revised Standard Version. Vocational root words are a small percentage (0.1 percent) of the OT.

In an examination of the 597 OT verses, only 149 English words (144 Hebrew words) are associated with God directing the action. For example, in Gen 1:10, God *calls* (קרא [*qr'*]) the dry land earth and the waters seas. In Gen 22:14, it is not God but Abraham who uses the same Hebrew root verb to name the place where he was tested by God "The Lord will provide." Only 25 percent of the OT vocational words are associated directly with God as the one doing the action. Of the eight different English vocational root words and their derivatives, 56 percent (eighty-four) are from the English vocational root "call" and are always associated with the uninflected Hebrew form קרא (*qr'*).

---

1. The New Revised Standard Version (NRSV), an English translation of the original Hebrew, Greek, and Aramaic texts, is quoted throughout this book, except where noted.

CHARISMATA

God performs four functions with the first English vocational root "call." (1) God *names* or *renames*. For example, in Gen 17:15, God renames Sarai to Sarah. There are thirty-two English verses in which God names or renames. In Hebrew Scripture, when God names something, it is more than just designating a label; it is to *be* something.[2] To name an object or living being is more than a simple title or practical identification. In Near Eastern thought, something did not exist prior to its being named. God creates through naming. The Genesis creation story brings order to the cosmos through God's naming.[3] For example, in Gen 1:5: "God called the light Day, and the darkness he called Night." (2) God *proclaims*. There are three English verses in which God proclaims. For example, in Hag 1:11, God proclaims a drought. (3) God *summons*. God summons individuals like Moses to the top of Mount Sinai (Exod 19:20). Being summoned by God can be "intensely personal" such as when God calls Samuel (1 Sam 3:4).[4] Even though individuals are summoned by God, they are still part of a community, a group of chosen people in a covenant relationship.[5] God summons groups of people like the Israelites (Isa 43:1), and God summons the material world as when God calls for waters in the sea (Amos 5:8). God's summoning has the highest English word count at fifty-four. (4) God *shouts* for a shower of fire in Amos 7:4, which is a form of summoning.

The second vocational English root word, "summon," is used in fifteen verses. In twelve verses, the NRSV translates the same Hebrew root "call" (קרא [*qrʾ*]) as God summons, in a similar way as the English vocational root "call." In two verses, Jer 50:29 and 51:27, a different Hebrew root is used (שמע [*šmʿ*]), which means "to hear or proclaim" but is translated into English as summoning archers and Israel. In another verse, Ps 68:28, a different Hebrew root (צוה [*ṣwh*]) is translated as "summon" but is a *request* for God's might.

2. Marshall, *Kind of Life*, 12.
3. Walton, *Ancient Near Eastern Thought*, 158–59; Walton, *Lost World*, 29.
4. Badcock, *Way of Life*, 4.
5. Kee and Shroyer, *Bible and God's Call*, 14–15.

Premodern (Creation to 1687)

In only one verse, Zech 3:10, the third English vocational root "invite" (קרא [qr']) is used by God to *ask* the Israelites to come under a vine and fig tree.

In only one verse, Num 16:9, the fourth English vocational root "separate" (בדל [bdl]) is used by God to *separate* the Levites for duties of the Lord's tabernacle.

In two verses, Deut 10:8 and 1 Chr 23:13, the fifth English vocational root "set apart" (בדל [bdl]) is used when God *sets apart* the tribe of Levi, Aaron, and his sons for ministerial duties, in a similar manner as the English vocational root "separate."

The sixth English vocational root, "made king" (מלך [mlk]), is found in seven verses. God *makes kings*: Saul (1 Sam 15:11, 35), Solomon (1 Kgs 3:7; 2 Chr 1:8, 9, 11), and David (1 Chr 28:4). In similar fashion, the seventh English vocational root, "anoints" (משח [mšḥ]), is found in eleven verses. For example, God *anoints* Jehu as king over Israel (2 Kgs 9:3, 6, 12) to destroy the house of Ahab (2 Chr 22:7).

In twenty-eight verses, the eighth and last English vocational root, "choose" (בחר [bḥr]), is used by God to *choose* individuals and groups for defined tasks such as ruling (David, Solomon) and ministering (Aaron, Eli's family, Levites). For example, God chooses David as king (1 Kgs 8:16) and does not choose his brothers (1 Sam 16:8–10). The tribe of Levi and his sons are chosen to carry the ark (1 Chr 15:2) and to minister (Deut 18:5).

After examining the English vocational root words and their associated derivatives, some interesting conclusions can be made. First, God did not call the Genesis patriarchs, at least not in the ways that Moses, Aaron, David, and the Israelites were called. "Call" is used in the book of Isaiah for Abraham (Isa 51:2) and Jacob/the Israelites (Isa 48:12). The Hebrew use of "call" came into use much later in time.[6] Second, God interacted almost exclusively with the Hebrews, his chosen people. Cyrus II of Persia (c. 600–530 BCE) was the exception as God called Cyrus "though you did not know me" (Isa 45:4). Cyrus (also named "bird of prey," "victor from the east," and "one from the north") prospered and subdued

---

6. Badcock, *Way of Life*, 4.

nations (Isa 41:2, 25; 45:1,3,4; 46:11; 48:15). And third, the number of individual people that were called by God in an unmistakable way during the long OT history was a minuscule percentage of the total number of God's chosen people. God's unmistakable calling of individuals was limited.[7] In the OT, God's call was more corporate: the community of Israel was God's people[8] dwelling in righteousness.[9]

God calls people to tasks, such as Moses to lead the Hebrews out of Egyptian bondage (Exod 3:4), Saul to be the first king of Israel (1 Sam 15:17), and Bezalel (with craftsmen) to build the tent of meeting and the ark of the covenant (Exod 31:1–11, 35:30—36:2). God used these people as mediators.[10] Most of these mediators were quietly working in various occupations and not actively seeking a leadership position. In fact, most were reluctant to serve, as the tasks were daunting and life threatening.[11] While leading the Israelites was a defined position, it wasn't a traditional job. However, craftsmen building the tabernacle was a traditional work task. This was the only instance in the OT of a non-ministerial/leadership task that God called people to perform. This Exodus occurrence was not a career position, just a special assignment.[12]

There is only one instance in the OT of God calling a person or a group of people to a full-time, paid career.[13] Aaron and his sons were anointed to be priests (Lev 7:35–36), and Aaron was chosen to be "the holy one" (Num 16:5, 7; Ps 105:26). Aaron was "set apart to consecrate the most holy things, so that he and his sons forever should make offerings before the Lord, and minister to him and pronounce blessings in his name forever" (1 Chr 23:13). The Aaronite order was given authority over the Levites (Num 3:5–10; 8:5–22). The tribe of Levi "and his sons for all time" were chosen

---

7. Christian History, "Gifts That Differ," 4; Badcock, *Way of Life*, 42–43.
8. Heiges, *Christian's Calling*, 31.
9. Marshall, *Kind of Life*, 12.
10. Schuurman, *Vocation*, 20.
11. Heiges, *Christian's Calling*, 31; Conyers, "Meaning of Vocation," 14.
12. Wong and Rae, *Business for Common Good*, 61.
13. Wong and Rae, *Business for Common Good*, 45.

PREMODERN (CREATION TO 1687)

to be priests, to be God's ministers, and to carry the ark (Deut 18:5; 21:5; 1 Chr 15:2; 2 Chr 29:11). Like Aaron and his sons, the tribe of Levi was separated from the congregation of Israel to perform the duties of the Lord's tabernacle (Num 16:9). The relationship between the Aaronite priestly order and the Levites had its share of power struggles (Num 16:1–11). When Solomon's Temple (First Temple) was destroyed by the Babylonian King Nebuchadnezzar II in 586 BCE, generational occupations of the Aaronites and Levites ended. The OT has almost no evidence of God calling his chosen people to specific occupations or careers, except for Aaron, the Levites, and their sons. God does state that the Hebrews "shall be for me a priestly kingdom and a holy nation" (Exod 19:6). This verse does not relate to a specific occupation nor a career, but ties back to the Hebrew corporate summons.

Searching the OT for verses that contain root words pertaining to gift or skill (uninflected Hebrew form and derivatives/cognates) produces 130 English words and 127 Hebrew words, 22 percent of the vocational words previously examined in the OT.

When examining these OT verses, only twenty-one English words (twenty-one Hebrew words) are associated with God's gifting. Examining these small number of verses with the root gift or skill, God performs three functions. (1) God is *benevolent*. This function is shown nine times in the OT. The meaning of gift is used in the traditional way. For example, God gives the gift (מֶגֶד [*meged*]) of land to the Israelites (Deut 33:13, 16). In Hebrew, the word literally means "excellent thing." As I previously discussed, God gives the gift (מַתָּנָה [*mattānāh*]) of the Levites to the Israelites (Num 18:6,7,19). (2) God commands the *use of skill*. This function occurs only once in the OT. God is not giving the skill (חשב [*maʿăśēh*]) but is commanding that the skill be used: "You shall make a breastpiece of judgment, in skilled work; you shall make it in the style of the ephod; of gold, of blue and purple and crimson yarns, and of fine twisted linen you shall make it" (Exod 28:15). The phrase "in skilled work" (מַעֲשֵׂה חֹשֵׁב [*maʿăśēh ḥošēb*]) literally means "work of a designer" or "work of planning." The same phrase appears in Exod 26:1, 31; 28:6; 36:8,35; and 39:3, 8. However, in these verses, the NRSV translates the Hebrew as "skillfully worked into them" or similar phrases. The Hebrew particle is functioning as a noun, indicating work that requires planning or knowledge. Yahweh is instructing that the tabernacle elements be made with the skill of a specialist. (3) God *endows with abilities*.[14] This function occurs the most (eleven words in nine verses). Except for one verse, all are in two different sections within Exodus.[15] The first section (Exod 28) concerns the priestly vestments: "And you shall speak to all who have ability, whom I have endowed with skill, that they make Aaron's vestments to consecrate him for my priesthood" (Exod 28:3). The noun (skill) literally means "wisdom" (חָכְמָה [ḥokmāh]), and here it is envisioned as wisdom for a task. The overall phrase "endowed with skill" is a combination of "wisdom" (חָכְמָה [ḥokmāh]) with "spirit" (רוּחַ [rûaḥ])—thus "whom I have filled with a spirit of wisdom."

The second Exodus section concerns the appointment of craftsmen (Exod 31:1–11; 35:30—36:7).[16] The Hebrew word for "wisdom" (חָכְמָה [ḥokmāh]) is used in six verses (Exod 31:3, 6; 35:31, 35; 36:1–2). Exodus 31:3 and 35:31 are of particular interest: "I/He [God] have/has filled him with divine spirit, with skill, intelligence, and knowledge in every kind of craft." The "divine spirit" can also be translated "the spirit of God." Skilled craftsmen are filled with the spirit of God. This parallels the New Testament Scripture that will be evaluated in the next section. As part of this spiritual endowment, God also gifts intelligence (תְּבוּנָה [təbûnāh]) and knowledge (דַּעַת [da'at]). Outside of this context, this combination of three qualities is in a description of Hiram of Tyre, who assisted in providing bronze implements for Solomon's Temple (1 Kgs 7:14), and in a list of qualities that can be sought from God in the pursuit of wisdom (Prov 2:6). Three verses in this section (Exod 31:6; 36:1–2) contain the Hebrew noun "wisdom" (חָכְמָה [ḥokmāh]) with the Hebrew noun "heart" (לֵב [lēb]) to indicate "one who is wise at heart for the task," thus skillful. A fourth instance of

---

14. Schuurman, *Vocation*, 31.
15. Heiges, *Christian's Calling*, 26.
16. Wong and Rae, *Business for Common Good*, 60.

this combination appears in Exod 35:35 to reference the divinely granted skill (literally "wise heart") that allows the workers to do the work necessary for the production of the tabernacle's implements: "He has filled them with skill [חָכְמַת־לֵב (ḥokmat-lēb)] to do every kind of work done by an artisan or by a designer or by an embroiderer in blue, purple, and crimson yarns, and in fine linen, or by a weaver—by any sort of artisan or skilled designer."

The one non-Exodus verse where God endows with abilities is Dan 1:17: "To these four young men [Daniel, Hananiah, Mishael, and Azariah] God gave knowledge and skill in every aspect of literature and wisdom; Daniel also had insight into all visions and dreams." Here God grants the four Hebrew boys both knowledge (מַדָּע [maddāʿ]) and skill (הַשְׂכֵּל [haśkēl]). The term for "skill" is an infinitive form of the Hebrew root שׂכל (śkl), which can denote both prudence and success. Thus, it is possible to say that God has given the young men abilities to be successful in the court of Babylon.

SCRIPTURE: NEW TESTAMENT

The story of vocation continues with Scripture in the New Testament (NT). The NRSV NT contains twenty-seven books with 176,424 words, about a third of the number of words that are in the OT. Searching the NRSV NT for verses that contain vocational words (uninflected Greek form and derivatives/cognates) produces 329 English words and 318 Greek words. Again, the small differences in the English and Greek word counts are between the translation and source texts. These five vocational words (call, choose, exhort, know, and summon) are a small percentage (0.2 percent) of the NRSV NT.

An examination of the NRSV NT verses shows that only sixty-four English words (sixty-three Greek words) are associated with God directing the action. For example, in Eph 1:18, God calls (καλέω [kaleō]) the "enlightened" Ephesians to "know what is the hope." In 2 Thess 2:14, God calls (καλέω [kaleō]) the Thessalonians to faith in Jesus Christ. Only 18 percent of the NRSV NT vocational words are directly associated with God as the one doing the action. Of the five vocational words and their derivatives, sixty-two (97 percent) are translated as "call," while the other two are translated as "invite" (καλέω [kaleō]) and "choose" (ἐκλεκτός [eklektos]). The English word "call" has four different Greek uninflected forms: καλέω (kaleō) with forty-five words (73 percent); κλῆσις (klēsis) with six words (10 percent); κλητός (klētos) with nine words (14 percent); and προσκαλέω (proskaleō) with two words (3 percent).

God performs five functions with three of the vocational words (call, invite, and choose). The first is that God *asks*, which is translated in only one verse (Rev 19:9) as "invite": God asks people "to the marriage supper of the Lamb." The Greek (καλέω [kaleō]) makes a strong case that it could have been translated as "call."

The second function is that God *chooses*. This is used only once (ἐκλεκτός [eklektos]) in 1 Pet 2:9, and within the same verse, the Greek "call" (καλέω [kaleō]) is also present. There exists a direct linkage of God's chosen people, Israel, with God's call to Jesus Christ.

The third function is that God *commands*, although the Greek is translated in the NRSV as "called." This is used once (Heb 11:8) when Abraham obeys the command of God to travel to the promised land. The same Greek form καλέω (kaleō) is used.

The fourth function is that God *names*. This occurs in three verses employing four vocational words. For example, Jesus quotes Isa 56:7 in Matt 21:13, "My [God's] house shall be called a house of prayer." The same Greek form (καλέω [kaleō]) is used.

The fifth and by far the most prevalent function (fifty-seven words) is that God *summons*. Unlike the other four functions, there are four different Greek forms used to summon: καλέω (kaleō) with forty words; κλῆσις (klēsis) with six words; κλητός (klētos) with nine words; and προσκαλέω (proskaleō) with two words. God summons individuals or groups of people to: holiness (Rom 1:7; 1 Cor 1:2; 1 Thess 4:7), faith in Jesus Christ (Rom 1:6; Phil 3:4; Jude 1:1), to proclaim the good news (Acts 16:10; 2 Thess 2:14), justification and sanctification (Rom 8:30; 1 Pet 2:9), eternal life (1 Tim 6:12; Heb 9:15), freedom (1 Cor 7:22; Gal 3:15; 5:13),

PREMODERN (CREATION TO 1687)

hope (Eph 1:18; 4:4), fellowship (1 Cor 1:9), peace (1 Cor 7:15; Col 3:15), his purpose (Rom 8:28), to be an apostle[17] (Rom 1:1; 1 Cor 1:1; Gal 1:15), and to lead the life assigned (1 Cor 7:17). As followers of Jesus Christ, God is calling people into a relationship with God that leads to salvation, a new way of life, and service.[18] People are "to be conformed to the image of his Son"[19] (Rom 8:29). "Whatever you do, do everything for the glory of God"[20] (1 Cor 10:31). *"The whole life of the Christian becomes, therefore, part and parcel of his vocation under God."*[21]

In one verse (Acts 13:2), the Holy Spirit summons and "sets apart" Barnabas and Saul "for the work to which I have called them." The Greek form is προσκαλέω (*proskaleō*). The Spirit calls them to spread the gospel to the gentiles.

Given that Jesus Christ is both fully human and fully divine, one must also investigate vocational words used by Jesus in the NT. There are three different vocational words and their derivatives that are associated with Jesus: call (forty-three), choose (one), and summon (one). In Rev 17:14, both "choose" (ἐκλεκτός [*eklektos*]) and "call" (κλητός [*klētos*]) are used in the same verse, which describes Jesus Christ as "the Lamb" and "those with him are called and chosen and faithful." In this verse, "call" and "choose" are interchangeable in meaning. In Matt 10:1, "Jesus summoned [προσκαλέω (*proskaleō*)] his twelve disciples." *Proskaleō* is the verb *kaleō* with the prefix *pros-*, which translates as "to call forward." "Summon" is more emphatic than "call," but it is the same command that is used to gather together Jesus's disciples, and translators could also have selected "call."

Jesus performs six functions with these three vocational words. The first is that Jesus *addresses* (προσφωνέω [*prosphōneō*]), which is translated in only one verse as "call": "he called his disciples and chose twelve of them" (Luke 6:13). *Prosphōneō* means

17. Paul S. Minear, in J. Nelson, *Work and Vocation*, 73.
18. Guinness, *Call*, 30; Stevens, *Doing God's Business*, 21–22.
19. Kee and Shroyer, *Bible and God's Call*, 61.
20. Groothuis, *Truth Decay*, 278.
21. Heiges, *Christian's Calling*, 40; emphasis original.

"to speak to." The Greek base, *phōneō*, means "to speak or utter a sound" with the prefix *pros-*, which means "to or towards." It is both verbal and special. Jesus is both speaking to his disciples and calling them towards him. The gathering of disciples was for a selection process.

The second function is that Jesus *chooses* (ἐκλέγω [*eklegō*]), also in Luke 6:13, which is a leadership action performed by Jesus. *Eklegō* is a compound Greek word with the base *legō*, meaning "choose" or "select," and the prefix *ek-*, meaning "out" or "away from."

The third function is that Jesus *names or renames*. For example, in Matt 5:9, Jesus names peacemakers "children of God," and in John 1:42, Jesus renames Simon, son of John, as Cephas. This function is used by Jesus in nine verses: eight verses with the Greek καλέω (*kaleō*) and one verse with λέγω (*legō*).

The fourth function is that Jesus *says* (καλέω [*kaleō*]). An example of this is found in Mark 10:18 and Luke 18:19: "Jesus said to him, 'Why do you call me good?'" The more precise translation is "Why do you say that I am good?" This has nothing to do with naming but refers to the adjective that describes Jesus.

The fifth function is that Jesus *shouts* (φωνέω [*phōneō*]). It is translated as "called," but in Luke 8:8 it literally means Jesus shouted.

The sixth function is that Jesus *summons*, which is used in thirty verses. Six different Greek forms are used, and except in the one verse previously described, all words are translated as "call": καλέω (*kaleō*) with six words; κλητός (*klētos*) with one word; προσκαλέω (*proskaleō*) with fourteen words; προσφωνέω (*prosphōneō*) with one word; φωνέω (*phōneō*) with seven words; and συγκαλέω (*sunkaleō*) with one word. Of the thirty NT verses containing Jesus's summoning, all but two are in the Gospels: Matthew (nine), Mark (thirteen), Luke (four), and John (two). Jesus summons his disciples (thirteen),[22] crowds (four), and sinners (three). He summons individuals: a child, a crippled woman, two blind men, Lazarus, Mary, James, and John. Jesus summons Elijah

---

22. Kee and Shroyer, *Bible and God's Call*, 32.

Premodern (Creation to 1687)

(two) from the cross. In 1 Pet 1:15, Jesus ("he who called you is holy") summons people to holiness. Jesus's summoning is not just a gathering of people, but a transformational change that results in actions: love of neighbors through service, possible suffering, and eternal life.[23] There are no instances of people successfully volunteering to be Jesus's disciple.[24] The summons is always *external* to the person being called.[25]

When comparing the NT vocational words with the OT, there are similarities. God and Jesus perform similar functions in both Testaments: naming/renaming, summoning, shouting, choosing, and asking. In the OT, God interacts almost exclusively with the Hebrews. In the NT, Jesus mainly follows this trend. After his death and resurrection, Jesus's followers spread the good news to both Jews and gentiles; God's summoning expands to all people. The OT summoning is more corporate (the Hebrew community of Israel),[26] while the NT is more personal,[27] yet also corporate (supranational, ecumenical community of the church).[28] Both Testaments call people to tasks. The OT has one incident of God calling a group of people to a full-time, paid career (Aaron and his sons, the tribe of Levites), which ends shortly after Jesus's death. The NT contains no examples of calling people to full-time, paid careers.[29] "The call of the gospel is not to a particular occupation, but to sainthood."[30] Vocation is primarily concerned with calling all to faith in Jesus Christ. It is living the Christian life by loving your neighbor and faithful obedience. Vocation is personal, something

---

23. Guinness, *Call*, 30.
24. Badcock, *Way of Life*, 5.
25. Conyers, "Meaning of Vocation," 13.
26. Conyers, "Meaning of Vocation," 15.
27. Richardson, *Biblical Doctrine of Work*, 34.
28. Heiges, *Christian's Calling*, 21,42; Conyers, "Meaning of Vocation," 16.
29. Guinness, *Call*, 49; Marshall, *Kind of Life*, 14; Christian History, "Gifts That Differ," 4; Richardson, *Biblical Doctrine of Work*, 33; Stevens, *Doing God's Business*, 35–36.
30. Hardy, *Fabric of This World*, 80.

that happens to an individual.[31] Its use is singular, as there is only one calling that comes to a Christian. It is also why Paul uses *klēsis* in 1 Cor 1:26 as the total body of Corinthian Christians.[32] Any other vocation is being less human than God demands.[33] It is interesting to note that the Greek word for "call," *klēsis*, is rooted in other English spiritual words: cleric, ecclesiastical, and church (*ekklesia*).[34]

Searching the NRSV NT for verses that contain words pertaining to "gift" (uninflected Greek form and derivatives/cognates) produces seventy-seven Greek words and seventy-two English words, a very small percentage (.004 percent) of all the NT words. The difference between the number of Greek and English words is due primarily to translation.

There are three functions that relate to gift. The first is *benevolence*. For example, in Eph 3:7, God gives the gift of grace: "Of this gospel I have become a servant according to the gift of God's grace that was given me by the working of his power." In Acts 10:45, the Holy Spirit is given as a gift to the gentiles: "The circumcised believers who had come with Peter were astounded that the gift of the Holy Spirit had been poured out even on the Gentiles." Jesus Christ, in Rev 21:6, gives the gift of life: "Then he said to me, 'It is done! I am the Alpha and the Omega, the beginning and the end. To the thirsty I will give water as a gift from the spring of the water of life.'" And Paul, in Rom 1:11, hopes to share with his Roman readers a spiritual gift: "For I am longing to see you so that I may share with you some spiritual gift to strengthen you." There are thirty-one Greek words (twelve different words in the uninflected form) and twenty-seven English words functioning as benevolence.

The second function is *donation*; all relate to a person or a group who gives gifts to another person, group, or God. A well-known example is found in Matt 2:11 when wise men from the

---

31. Conyers, "Meaning of Vocation," 17.
32. Holl, "History of Word *Vocation*," 127.
33. Badcock, *Way of Life*, 10, 13.
34. Conyers, "Meaning of Vocation," 12.

east give gifts to the baby Jesus: "On entering the house, they saw the child with Mary his mother; and they knelt down and paid him homage. Then, opening their treasure chests, they offered him gifts of gold, frankincense, and myrrh." Another donation example is when Paul collects money for the poor in Jerusalem: "So I thought it necessary to urge the brothers to go on ahead to you, and arrange in advance for this bountiful gift that you have promised, so that it may be ready as a voluntary gift and not as an extortion" (2 Cor 9:5). There are twenty-seven Greek (twelve different uninflected form) words and twenty-seven English gift words associated with donation.

The third function is *talent*, which relates to vocation. These are abilities that individuals possess. There are only nineteen Greek (seven different uninflected form) words and eighteen English words, about 25 percent of all the gift words, located in only eighteen verses within seven books of the NT. First Corinthians contains eleven of the verses (61 percent), the majority in chs. 12 and 14. Chapter 13 is also part of this section on spiritual gifts, but there are no gift words within this chapter. The Gospels do not contain any references to gifts that function as talents.

Starting in biblical order, Acts has one verse (21:9) that uses gift as talent. Philip, the evangelist, has four unmarried daughters with the gift (προφητεύω [*prophēteuō*]) of prophecy. This is the only time this Greek word functions as talent in the NT. This Greek word means "to be a prophet/preacher" and has a more specific context, but may be linked to spiritual gifts, considering it is associated with Paul as he journeys to Jerusalem.

Paul's Letter to the Romans contains a short section (12:3–8) about the holy life and parallels 1 Cor 12–14. Romans 12:6 is translated: "We have gifts [δίδωμι (*didōmi*)] that differ according to the grace given to us: prophecy, in proportion to faith." Grace (χάρις [*charis*]) is also a Greek word for "gift." Thus, two Greek words for "gift" are in this verse but only one directly relates to talent. I include both words in the talent word count since the words are linked. Paul lists seven general talents that are God-given (Rom 12:6–8): prophecy, ministry, teaching, exhorting, giving, leading, and compassion. Paul ties these spiritual talents to the body of Christ; however, some of these talents can be used in non-spiritual settings in service to others.[35]

Paul's First Letter to the Corinthians is the bulk of his writings about spiritual talents. Just after Paul's greeting (1:1–3) to the Corinthians, Paul states that Christ Jesus has "enriched" the Corinthians "in speech and knowledge of every kind" (1:5), "so that you are not lacking in any spiritual gift [χάρισμα (*charisma*)] as you wait for the revealing of our Lord Jesus Christ" (1:7). *Charisma* is derived from *charis*, and Paul's use is the first instance in biblical Greek writings. In 3:1—4:21, Paul admonishes the Corinthians for their spiritual immaturity. Their boasting of their talents led Paul to write in 1 Cor 4:7: "For who sees anything different in you? What do you have that you did not receive? And if you received it, why do you boast as if it were not a gift [λαμβάνω (*lambanō*)]?" Paul does not use *charisma* in this verse. A more literal translation of 1 Cor 4:7 is: "For who distinguished you [from someone else]? What do you have that you did not receive [*lambanō*]? And if you received [*lambanō*] it, why do you boast that you did not receive [*lambanō*]?" *Lambanō* means "to take, seize, grasp; receive" and could mean to receive a gift but could also mean to receive something else. It's not specific to gift or etymologically related to any words for "gift." Although I include it in the talent word count, it is doubtful that Paul specifically refers to talent.

In 1 Cor 7:1–40, Paul discusses marriage and sexual relations. Paul advises, but does not command, married couples not to practice celibacy "because of your lack of self-control" (7:5). "I [Paul] wish that all were as I myself am. But each has a particular gift [χάρισμα (*charisma*)] from God, one having one kind and another a different kind" (7:7). Paul ties celibacy to a talent given by God.

The remainder of 1 Corinthians gift words reside in chs. 12 and 14. This well-known section of Paul's letter is superb prose. Paul addresses the issue of speaking in tongues within the Corinthian church, but Paul also includes other talents. God created all in God's image, but each person has unique talents. Humans were

---

35. Doriani, *Work*, 94.

Premodern (Creation to 1687)

created with different talents, but in Jesus Christ, the differences become irrelevant.[36] Paul opens with this statement: "Now concerning spiritual [πνευμάτικος (*pneumatikos*)] gifts, brothers and sisters, I do not want you to be uninformed" (12:1). Paul uses the word *pneumatikos* as a neuter adjective (plural: *pneumatika*). A literal translation is "spiritual *things*." The NRSV translator chose to add "gifts" after "spiritual," but gifts are not explicit in the Greek text; however, it is reasonable to imply gifts since Paul elaborates on the work of the Spirit throughout the chapter. Just a few verses later (12:4), Paul ties gifts to the Spirit: "Now there are varieties of gifts [χάρισμα (*charisma*; plural: *charismata*)], but the same Spirit." Paul then writes in 12:8–11 of various forms of talents, the majority relating to spiritual gifts: faith, healing, working of miracles, prophecy, discernment of spirits, various kinds and interpretation of tongues. The utterance of wisdom and knowledge may be spiritual or not, although all talents come from the Spirit. In 12:14–26, Paul illustrates examples of gifts to the larger community by using the human body as a metaphor.[37]

In 1 Cor 12:27–31, Paul states that "God has appointed in the church" (12:28) "the body of Christ and individually members of it" (12:27) to various church offices (apostles, prophets, teachers, the powerful, healers, assistance givers, leaders, tongue speakers, and interpreters). Paul consistently uses the same Greek words for "gift" (χάρισμα [*charisma*]) in vv. 12:28, 30, and 31. The gifts are spiritual gifts because these gifts are linked to the body of Christ, the church. However, several of the talents can be used outside the religious community.[38] Paul describes individual gifts, but the various talents are to be used *within* and *for* community, which is the body of Christ.[39]

Chapter 14 contains the remaining two gift words found in 1 Corinthians. Paul opens this chapter with: "Pursue love and strive for the spiritual [πνευμάτικος (*pneumatikos*)] gifts, and especially

---

36. Brunner, *Christianity and Civilisation*, 118.
37. Volf, *Work in the Spirit*, 190.
38. Schuurman, *Vocation*, 143.
39. Schuurman, *Vocation*, 123–24.

that you may prophesy" (14:1). As in 12:1, gifts are implied, but it is reasonable to insert "gifts" since this section is about spiritual gifts. The final usage of the word "gift" as a talent is in 14:12: "So with yourselves; since you are eager for spiritual gifts [πνευμάτικος (*pneumatikos*)], strive to excel in them for building up the church." This is the third example of implying gifts after the word "spiritual," consistent with the other two examples.

In Paul's Letter to the Ephesians, Paul writes about Christ giving "gifts [δόμα (*doma*)] to his people" (4:8). There is another Greek word for "gift" in this verse: "gave" (δίδωμι [*didōmi*]). This verse in isolation does not link to talent. However, 4:8 is linked to 4:11 with the same Greek uninflected form word for "gift": "The gifts [δίδωμι (*didōmi*)] he gave were that some would be apostles, some prophets, some evangelists, some pastors and teachers." The next verse (4:12) identifies these gifts as spiritual: "to equip the saints for the work of ministry, for building up the body of Christ." The list of roles is within the church, the body of Christ.

Paul's First Letter to Timothy has only one verse with gifts used as talent. Paul contrasts the differences between true and false teaching (1 Tim 4:1—5:2). Paul writes in 1 Tim 4:14: "Do not neglect the gift [χάρισμα (*charisma*)] that is in you, which was given to you through prophecy with the laying on of hands by the council of elders." What gift was Timothy neglecting? Paul gives a general hint in 4:13: "Give attention to the public reading of Scripture, to exhorting, to teaching." These talents are spiritual and roles within the church.[40] As in Eph 4:8, 1 Tim 4:14 has the same second Greek word for "gift" (δίδωμι [*didōmi*]), which is translated as "given." Paul refers to this same theme in 2 Tim 1:6: "For this reason I remind you to rekindle the gift [χάρισμα (*charisma*)] of God that is within you through the laying on of my hands." The difference between the two letters is that Paul uses *charisma* instead of *didōmi*.

The last NT book in which gift functions as a talent is in 1 Peter, "Like good stewards of the manifold grace [χάρισμα (*charisma*)] of God, serve one another with whatever gift [χάρις (*charis*)]

---

40. Higginson, *Questions of Business Life*, 261.

each of you has received" (4:10). Peter speaks of two ordinary talents,[41] speaking and serving, and does not link these talents to the church, but states only that the gift comes from God through grace.

God's gifts/talents to individuals are related to vocation as the *how*: glorifying God[42] by loving one's neighbor as God commands. Christians, using their God-given talents, are God's stewards on earth.[43] Specifically, the NT does not contain an individualistic formula to determine how to use God-given talents. Scripture states only that talents are gifts from God, given in love to love,[44] and lists various roles that are primarily within the church. While the NT, mainly through Paul's letters, focuses on spiritual gifts, the NT does not state that gifts are exclusive to spiritual matters. It is reasonable, by extension, that God's gifts can be used in all forms of daily life. More on this will follow in the section on Miroslav Volf.

SCRIPTURE: THE "PROBLEM" TEXT (1 COR 7:17–24)

There are troublesome texts within Scripture. For example, verses can be interpreted out of context, translations from Hebrew and Greek into English may be inaccurate or untranslatable, and historical cultural settings may mask meanings in our postmodern culture. Much ink has been shed on 1 Cor 7:17–24 since the Reformation. It is a key vocational text, yet has perplexed many Christians, especially since the industrial age has greatly changed the work culture.

Throughout this book, I have consistently used the NRSV. However, for this section, I will use the 1 Cor 7:17–24 translation found in *The First Epistle to the Corinthians*, edited by Gordon D. Fee. Here is the text:

---

41. Wolters, *Creation Regained*, 105–6.
42. Groothuis, *Truth Decay*, 278; Heiges, *Christian's Calling*, 79.
43. Troeltsch, *Social Teaching*, 1:77.
44. Badcock, *Way of Life*, 123.

> [17] Nevertheless, each person should live as a believer in whatever situation the Lord has assigned to them, just as God has called them. This is the rule I lay down in all the churches. [18] Was a man already circumcised when he was called? He should not become uncircumcised. Was a man uncircumcised when he was called? He should not be circumcised. [19] Circumcision is nothing and uncircumcision is nothing. Keeping God's commands is what counts. [20] Each person should remain in the situation they were in when God called them.
>
> [21] Were you a slave when you were called? Don't let it trouble you—although if you can gain your freedom, do so. [22] For the one who was a slave when called to faith in the Lord is the Lord's freed person; similarly, the who was free when called is Christ's slave. [23] You were bought at a price; do not become slaves of human beings. [24] Brothers and sisters, each person, as responsible to God, should remain in the situation they were in when God called them.[45]

These eight verses inserted into ch. 7 are part of the chapter that discusses marriage. In 7:1–16 and 7:25–40, Paul writes to the Corinthian Christians about sexual relations, divorce, remarriage, and relations within marriage. These issues were sparking controversy in the Corinthian church. Paul begins ch. 7 by discussing sexual immorality conducted by Corinthian Christians. He advises the married faithful not to practice abstinence, which he hoped would curb their immorality (7:1–7). Paul counsels widowers and widows to either remain single or marry, if they cannot control their sexual urges (7:8–9). He forbids divorce if both are Christians (7:10–11) and applies the same prohibition for mixed marriages (7:12–16). In 7:15, Paul states: "God has called us to live in peace." He connects this theme with 7:17–24.

Another Corinthian church controversy was that converted members were changing their social status to conform to their new spiritual lives as Christians. Paul interjects macro-theology into his micro-writings on marriage. God's call to faith in Christ (1

---

45. Fee, *First Epistle to Corinthians*, 339.

Premodern (Creation to 1687)

Cor 1:9) has nothing to do with social status, but rather with *whom* one belongs to. The change that occurs is a person's relationship with God, not with human societal constructions.[46]

Verse 7:17 adheres to the 7:1–16 theme: stay in your current social setting after your conversion. Vocation (calling), during Paul's writings, was a person's whole life, not his or her occupation.[47] Paul was not advocating remaining forever in their social setting but believed that the Corinthians could live out God's call just as they were when called by God. Their current social status was sanctified; no change was required. God's calling has nothing to do with occupations;[48] it is a gracious gift that requires nothing in return.[49] To emphasize v. 17, Paul cites in 7:18–19 another issue within the Corinthian church: circumcision. He applies the same theological stance: stay as you are. Perhaps it was Paul's own conversion experience on the road to Damascus that constructed his theology. Paul came to Christ suddenly after an encounter with the risen Jesus. Circumcision had nothing to do with Paul's calling.[50] For a Jew to say that "circumcision is nothing" was remarkable. This shows that Paul's highest priority was his calling to faith in Jesus Christ. God's calling is transformational;[51] it exceeds human works.

Equally remarkable is Paul's final statement in 7:19: "Keeping God's commands is what counts." Circumcision was commanded by God (Gen 17:10–14). However, Paul does not equate works, such as circumcision, as "God's command." In the Corinthian Christian community, where the behaviors of the minority Christians differed little from the pagan majority, Paul did not want the Corinthians to leap from not having to be circumcised to antinomian behavior. Paul was trying to balance his dualistic theology.[52]

---

46. Fee, *First Epistle to Corinthians*, 340.
47. Veith, "Vocation," 42.
48. Marshall, *Kind of Life*, 14.
49. Fee, *First Epistle to Corinthians*, 342–4.
50. Fee, *First Epistle to Corinthians*, 345–6.
51. Mackenzie and Kirkland, *Where's God on Monday*, 72.
52. Fee, *First Epistle to Corinthians*, 347.

Verse 7:20, which is so often quoted in vocational writings, reiterates Paul's views that Christians should not change their situation but remain *when* called.[53] If Paul uses "call" (χαλέω [*kaleō*]) as God summoning people to an external condition rather than to faith in Jesus Christ, then this interpretation occurs nowhere else in the New Testament or the Greek literature up to Paul's time. This would have been a first instance and highly unlikely.[54]

In vv. 21–23, Paul uses another micro-example of a Corinthian church issue: slavery. This issue is clouded by our postmodern societal views on slavery and racial injustice. Greco-Roman slaves were at the bottom of the social hierarchy when Paul wrote his letters. However, Greco-Roman slaves had more freedom than American slaves and benefited from steady employment, unlike the free day laborers who had no security. The social conditions of slaves in comparison to free day laborers were not that different. Paul minimalizes all social statuses by exchanging slavery for freedom in Christ and transforming free Christians into slaves of Christ. A free person could become a slave, but a slave could not, by themselves, become free. Paul places God's call above a person's situation or outward state of life,[55] even slavery. Don't be concerned with your situation at the time of your calling. In 7:23, a slave is free, and a free person is a slave, because both have been bought with the price of Jesus's blood on the cross.

It is important to highlight that Paul is writing about marriage, circumcision, and slavery, not secular employment, which is not even mentioned as an example.[56] Most likely, work was not an issue in Corinth, a prosperous commercial city. Paul never states that his tent-making occupation was a calling.[57] Moreover, Paul instructs slaves to gain their freedom "if you can" (1 Cor 7:21). He instructs single people to remain single unless "they cannot

---

53. Badcock, *Way of Life*, 7.

54. Stevens, *Doing God's Business*, 35–36; Marshall, *Kind of Life*, 14; Badcock, *Way of Life*, 8.

55. Robert L. Calhoun, in J. Nelson, *Work and Vocation*, 89.

56. Fee, *First Epistle to Corinthians*, 348–54.

57. Heiges, *Christian's Calling*, 38.

control themselves" (1 Cor 7:9). He tells mixed marriage couples to stay married and not divorce, "but if the unbeliever leaves, let it be so" (1 Cor 7:15). Paul's writings are not static and absolute, but flexible.[58] We do not know if there were other controversies in the Corinthian church that Paul does not mention in his letter,[59] but Paul was not against change in social status if there were good reasons for change. Another factor that overrides Paul's theology is time. In 7:29–31, Paul writes that "time is short" and "the world in its present form is passing away."[60] Why change if Jesus Christ is soon returning, perhaps in a few years, and the earthly life will be no more?[61] If Christ was shortly returning, then Paul did not anticipate the ongoing fellowship of the church where billions have been discipled. Paul might have modified his letter with a multigenerational vision.[62]

In 7:24, Paul echoes the same imperative stated in 7:17 and 7:20: a Christian's situation is sanctified when God calls. His letter requests that the Corinthian Christians, after accepting God's call, not dissolve their marriages or become celibate within marriages. A Christian's relationship with God is irrelevant to their social status. A believer can follow God's commands in whatever social situation exists at the time of their calling.[63] Dietrich Bonhoeffer (1906–45), German theologian and Lutheran pastor, reconciled Jesus's calling of the disciples to follow him (Mark 1:16–20) and Paul telling the Corinthians to "remain in the situation they were in when God called them" (1 Cor 7:20) by stating that the risen Lord (Holy Spirit) is present over all the earth through the sacraments; therefore, there is no need to leave everything, like the disciples who followed Jesus. Christians are with Christ through word and sacrament.[64]

58. Doriani, *Work*, 69.
59. Schuurman, *Vocation*, 32–33.
60. Fee, *First Epistle to Corinthians*, 369.
61. Robert L. Calhoun, in J. Nelson, *Work and Vocation*, 89.
62. Kee and Shroyer, *Bible and God's Call*, 62.
63. Fee, *First Epistle to Corinthians*, 355–6.
64. Bonhoeffer, *Cost of Discipleship*, 259.

This problematic text became foundational in Martin Luther's theology of vocation. Sadly, it took hundreds of years to repair a major Reformation theological mistake.

MONASTICISM

The New Testament was written within one hundred years of Jesus's death. During this period and afterwards, the idea of the kingdom of God had merged with the Christian church. Jesus's ushering in the kingdom was replaced by the exaltation of the church.[65] During the apostolic age, small groups of former Jews and gentiles met informally in homes, outside, or in public buildings to sing, read the Gospels and Paul's letters, celebrate the Lord's Supper, and baptize converts. Leaders were elected to plan, organize, and advise. As the movement grew in numbers, it became necessary for leaders to devote more time to the church. Eventually, a professional clergy was started, and worship services became more structured within erected buildings.

Our contemporary view of vocation, derived primarily from the Middle Ages and the Reformation, had no meaning in the early church. The social distinctions were present in trade and class, but within religious circles, Christians did away with these distinctions, and equal status was granted to all. The reason for this was that before original sin, there was original equality; there was no value in vocation or calling. After the fall, sinful humanity created divisions. Christians were more concerned about the coming kingdom. Thus, Paul's message to the Corinthians in his first letter (7:17–24) resonated with early Christians, the majority being lower middle class. This duality—external inequality existing with internal equality—held together when coupled with predestination and an eschatological focus. Vocation was derived from "fate" or "destiny," thus something to be criticized or regarded with indifference.[66]

---

65. Troeltsch, *Social Teachings*, 1:113.
66. Troeltsch, *Social Teachings*, 1:121–22.

PREMODERN (CREATION TO 1687)

As Christianity grew and normalized within the Roman state, the disconnection between God's call (*klēsis*) to faith in Christ and the non-Christian Roman state began to fade with the rise of infant baptism in the second century. An adult making a personal decision transitioned into something one was born into.[67]

The early church never contemplated the unity of church and state. Until the Roman emperor Constantine the Great (272–337 CE) issued the Edict of Milan in 313 CE legalizing Christianity, the church went through periods of persecution and legal bans. Christians could not work in any employment connected with pagan worship: temple artisans, military, temple services, judges, etc. In 323 CE, the once-despised religion became the state religion of the Roman Empire, a remarkable feat that the early Christians in Scripture had never predicted or sought. As early as 315 CE, Christian theology began to separate into two Christian classes: spiritual (above nature, perfection) and secular (humble, human).[68] Some Christians sought solitude by escaping the evil state. They lived ascetically, devoted to spiritual practices that demanded God be constantly before the soul. St. Anthony (252–356) is an early example. A monk would leave his previous life and all his sins behind, then be baptized a second time to lead a worthier life. This movement ran counter to the New Testament's theology of loving one's neighbor and spreading the gospel. These dedicated Christians failed to understand that it is impossible to escape culture; from birth, humans are a product of culture and still depend on it, whether they realize it or not.[69] The early church solitary movement was still not viewed as a vocational system "ordained by God and destined to contribute its part to the supreme religious meaning of life."[70]

While the Greek language dominated Eastern Christianity, Latin dominated the Western Church. Between 382 and 405 CE, St. Jerome translated the Hebrew Old Testament and the Greek

---

67. Holl, "History of Word *Vocation*," 128.
68. Heiges, *Christian's Calling*, 43–44.
69. Niebuhr, *Christ and Culture*, 72–76.
70. Troeltsch, *Social Teachings*, 1:123.

Charismata

New Testament into Latin. The result of this monumental task, named *the Vulgate*, was the primary biblical text until the Reformation. It is here that the English word "vocation" has its roots. The Greek word for "call," *klēsis*, was translated by Jerome into the Latin noun *vocatio* (verb: *vocare*). Jerome was consistent in his Greek translation and used the word 1,382 times in the Vulgate. Prior to his publication, *vocatio* was not commonly used in classical Latin. Its earliest use was in the first century BCE, and it was defined, at that time, as an invitation or military summons. In the second century CE, it was used as a legal summons. Tertullian (155–220), the father of Latin Christianity, translated *klēsis* as *vocatio*, so Jerome's was the first biblical translation. It must be noted that the early fathers of the church did not define *vocatio* in their writing as an occupation.[71] Its earlier uses were by the elite, while Jerome was publishing for a more general audience and parallels modern definitions.[72]

Once sanctioned by the state, the church blossomed into a bureaucracy. Church leaders, such as popes and bishops, became powerful and rivaled state leaders, who gave the church land and money for buildings. Unlike the solitary ascetics, church professionals banded together into religious communities to separate from the majority population who labored, which currently is called secular work. Christianity grew rapidly, and Christians started integrating into jobs that were previously deemed unacceptable. The difference was that paganism declined, and Christians started administering rules that favored Christianity. Christians thrust themselves into a sinful world, and their employment remained unconnected with their religious beliefs.[73]

Over hundreds of years, the New Testament theology of vocation changed. Vocation was assigned solely to religious occupations.[74] Only those secluded within monastic life as church

---

71. Holl, "History of Word *Vocation*," 136.
72. Rebecca Moorman, email to author, July 9, 2020.
73. Troeltsch, *Social Teachings*, 1:125–26.
74. Crouch, *Culture Making*, 256.

professionals, such as priests, monks, and nuns, had a vocation.[75] As early as Eusebius of Caesarea (260–339 CE), segregation was happening. Eusebius wrote about the "perfect life (*vita contemplativa*)" reserved for church professionals and "permitted life (*vita activa*)" that was reserved for everyone else. "Having a vocation" also meant living a celibate life.[76] St. John Cassian (c. 360–435), a Romanian monk and admirer of Anthony, wrote about the three stages of a monk's exclusive calling.[77] The spiritual and secular theological divide was starting to gain momentum. These divisions were not based on Scripture but were derived from human social structures.

Dr. H. Richard Niebuhr (1894–1962), Yale professor of theology, labeled this separation "Christ against culture" or "radical Christians."[78] The church, in theory, rejected the societal culture since it did not focus solely on spiritual matters. Cloistered spiritual communities created rules, such as *The Rule of St. Benedict* (c. 530), that dictated the perfect Christian life. St. Benedict (480–547) believed that art and trade jeopardized the soul of the monk. This temptation would be removed if the monks adhered to his orderly spiritual life.[79] Those in non-church professions worked to free church professionals for contemplation.[80] The monks and nuns organized and, through hard work, developed their lands and built massive structures. Through separation from non-church professions, a tiered hierarchy or caste system emerged: clergy (highest), nobility, craftsmen/peasants, and merchants/bankers (lowest).[81] Only a monk had a calling, thus merging God's call with a profession.[82] Equal rights, as we understand this ideal in our postmodern society, was an unknown concept.

75. Veith, *God at Work*, 17–19.
76. Whelchel, *How Then*, 54–63.
77. Holl, "History of Word *Vocation*," 132.
78. Niebuhr, *Christ and Culture*, 40–81.
79. Holl, "History of Word *Vocation*," 137.
80. Marshall, *Kind of Life*, 22.
81. Marshall et al., *Labour of Love*, 22.
82. Holl, "History of Word *Vocation*," 131.

The relationship between the state and church, although strained, was symbiotic: the state developed with the support of the church, and the church was supported by the state. Kings were anointed by church professionals. State wars were blessed by the church. This unity of church and state, along with the unique blend of social, economic, and political conditions, created the medieval Christian civilization.[83] This hierarchical system, with all its inherent inequalities, served to maintain order. Remaining within your station or caste preserved the organization. Individual freedoms within the lower stations presented a threat to the few who occupied the higher stations.[84] It was not the New Testament theology of vocation that was inserted into the premodern Christian culture, but the medieval culture was grafted onto the New Testament.[85]

For most of the Christian population (slaves, peasants, craftsmen), there was passive acceptance of their fate within their assigned station. The church taught their flock that the omnipotent God appointed their station at birth, and they should humbly and patiently accept it. Acquiescence was their calling, and those who tried to disrupt the hierarchy were duly punished.[86]

Economic traditionalism, present during medieval times, was "a *frame of mind* in respect to work. Work is viewed as a necessary evil and only one arena of life, no more important than the arenas of leisure, family, and friends." When basic needs were met, work ceased. This type of economy is in opposition to modern capitalism.[87] The medieval church generally "maintained a highly negative image of merchants and businessmen. Their perceived lust for gain placed riches above the kingdom of God and thereby endangered the soul, and their exploitation of persons on behalf of economic gain opposed the Christian ethic of brotherhood and group solidarity. An unequivocal axiom prevailed. . . . The merchant may

---

83. Troeltsch, *Social Teachings*, 1:246–56.
84. Troeltsch, *Social Teachings*, 1:290–91.
85. Troeltsch, *Social Teachings*, 1:294–95.
86. Troeltsch, *Social Teachings*, 1:296.
87. Weber, *Protestant Ethic*, 418; emphasis original.

conduct himself without sin but cannot be pleasing to God." Only the church professions, such as monks and nuns, organized their lives in a methodical-rational manner found in modern capitalism.[88] It took time for this systematic and disciplined lifestyle to be embraced by those outside of the spiritual professions.

By the late scholastic period, St. Berthold of Regensburg (c. 1220–72), a Franciscan monk, had divided the human social order into nine angelic choirs. The top three were ruling choirs: the pope with the priests, the monks, and then the secular rulers (kings, lords, and knights). The remaining six choirs were secular offices. These lower choirs served and gave provisions to sustain the higher choirs. In return, the spiritual offices prayed for the lower offices, thus mutually supporting each other in their distinct ways. The story of Martha and Mary (Luke 10:38–42) was used as scriptural support since Jesus states that "Mary has chosen the better part." Excluded from the choirs were those occupations not aligned with Christian character, like usurers and prostitutes, which were ruled by the devil.

Thomas Aquinas (1225–74), an Italian Dominican theologian, supported this division of labor. He believed that individuals in spiritual occupations must be totally dedicated to their tasks and supported by those in the lower, secular occupations. Thomas did not support the theology that God called people to their occupations and believed that social roles came from natural causes: God-given gifts to humans.[89]

It was German mysticism, founded between 1339 and 1343 in Switzerland, that started to mend the theological spiritual-secular divide. Mystics turned inward to find God, something all could achieve. The highest title, the friend of God, applied to both monastics and laity. Meister Eckhart (1260–1328) interpreted 1 Cor 7:20 as not everyone having the same calling by God; one can find God in all social roles. Therefore, he advocated that individuals remain in their current class.

---

88. Weber, *Protestant Ethic*, 24.
89. Holl, "History of Word *Vocation*," 138–40.

Johannes Tauler (c. 1300–1361), a Dominican disciple of Eckhart, did not enjoy being a monk and would have preferred a different occupation. He believed that he could achieve the same spiritual closeness to God without being a priest. However, the German mystics still insisted that monasticism was the highest occupation and preferred by God, based on obedience and renunciation. The German mystics helped elevate secular occupations during the late Middle Ages. Gabriel Biel (c. 1420–95), a German scholastic and philosopher, extended the title *religiosus* to professions approved by the church. Other German preachers informed their laity that their occupations were blessed, and they could gain heaven through them.[90]

Progress for individuals was limited to spiritual perfection.[91] The church taught that prayer, upholding the commandments, confession of sins, and performing prescribed penance would result in a Christian's eventual passage into heaven. The formula was straightforward: confession relieved the sinner's guilty burden, penance mitigated the damage, and the priest negated the sinful issue. This formula brought comfort and certainty to medieval Christians. Later, certainty of salvation became a theological and economic issue.

MARTIN LUTHER (1483-1546)

Theological cracks began to emerge when Western European education was revived in the eleventh century. Wandering teachers eventually assimilated into educational centers in the major European cities. The first was the University of Bologna (1088), followed by Paris (1150), Oxford (1200), Cambridge (1209), and Salamanca (1218). These academic centers trained the clergy and collected manuscripts that were dispersed throughout Christendom. The Vulgate was the only church-authorized version of the Bible. Since almost all the population was illiterate and could not

---

90. Holl, "History of Word *Vocation*," 141–44.
91. Douglas, "Talent and Vocation," 266.

read or speak Latin, the church controlled theology. Concentrated and organized learning centers were vehicles for theological debate, questioning of dogma, and change.

Peter Waldo (1140–1205) commissioned monks to translate the New Testament into his vernacular Romance language of Southern France. John Wycliffe (1328–84), a seminary professor at the University of Oxford, translated the Vulgate into Middle English. Jan Hus (1370–1415), a Czech theologian and graduate of Charles University (Prague), was influenced by Wycliffe's writings. He started questioning church theology and, through his scholarship, revealed differences between Scripture and church practices. He denounced clergy immorality, indulgences, and the church doctrine of the Eucharist. His education gave him the tools to challenge authority, but not the power to escape his cruel death by the Council of Constance. What was needed was a brilliant academic, astute marketer, and state protection. Martin Luther was perfect for the job.

Luther was born into a merchant mining family. His father was a leaseholder of copper mines and smelters. Luther grew up in the village of Eisleben, part of the Holy Roman Empire, and located today in eastern Germany. His father, observing his son's scholastic gifts, invested in private schools with the hope that Luther would become a lawyer. The combination of living in a working-class family and obtaining a good education served Luther well in marketing his theological concepts to the general population.

Luther continued his legal studies until 1505 when he was knocked off his horse by a lightning strike during a rainstorm. He asked St. Anne (Jesus's grandmother) to save him and pledged to become a monk. Luther survived and entered St. Augustine's Monastery in Erfurt where he became a super monk. He was so passionately dedicated and ascetic that his self-imposed hardships probably shortened his life. His superiors decided that he needed a change, so they transferred him to the University of Wittenberg where he eventually obtained a doctor of theology. In nearby Mainz, the printing press was invented by Johannes Gutenberg (1400–1468), which exponentially increased the number and affordability of published books. Thus, two of the three criteria for gaining theological changes were met by 1517, the year Luther nailed his Ninety-Five Theses on the Wittenberg University church door. This small academic act of defiance eventually snowballed into a Reformation that still impacts Christianity today.

Luther still needed a third attribute, state protection, and Prince Frederick III (1463–1525), elector of Saxony, provided it. The Holy Roman emperor Charles V (1500–1558) supported Rome's theological positions, yet politically needed Frederick's support. Frederick protected Luther because he wanted the University of Wittenberg to prosper, and Luther was his star professor. In 1521, Luther was provided safe travel to the Diet of Worms, where his writings were questioned. Luther refused to retract and was outlawed. Frederick kidnapped Luther during his travel back to Wittenberg and hid him in Wartburg Castle near Eisenach. Over the winter in a small castle room, Luther translated the New Testament into German, his vernacular language. This gave the local population access to Scripture in German through the new printing presses. Luther published many theological pamphlets, letters, and books during his lifetime and was what we call today a "bestseller." He understood the German population and brilliantly marketed his theological concepts, which were well received, as German Bibles were now available to the growing literate population.

Luther based his theology on Scripture, which countered church traditions. His most celebrated clash with the Church of Rome was on *sola fide*, that salvation comes only through faith in Christ. Believers did not need to perform works, such as the cycle of prayer, upholding the commandments, confession of sins, and performing prescribed penance, to achieve salvation after death. He did subscribe to election, God's choosing people to enjoy the benefits of salvation and to carry out God's purposes in the world, but did not emphasize it.

He countered the church's vocational hierarchy (spiritual over secular) with 1 Pet 2:9 ("But you are a chosen race, a royal priesthood, a holy nation"); all vocations that serve our neighbors are equal before God, thus affirming a universal priesthood.[92] In our postmodern culture, vocation is synonymous with occupation. But in Luther's culture, his radical redefinition of vocation uplifted Christians who did not serve professionally in the church.[93] Vocation applies to ecclesiastical *and* secular activities.[94] People did not have to join a religious order to have a vocation. They *already* had a vocation.[95] Priests do not exist in isolation, but in service to others.[96] All callings that uplifted the community were equally valued by God.

To understand Luther's doctrine of vocation, vocabulary is important. Luther translated "calling" (Greek: *klēsis*) into *Beruf* (German), which first appeared in his 1522 sermon of the *Kirchenpostille*.[97] *Beruf* is defined as an outer status or occupation. For example, the heading *Name, Vorname, Beruf*—last name, first name, occupation—appears on modern German application forms.[98] A second key vocabulary word is *Stand* (German), which translates into English as "station" and is synonymous with duty, estate, and office. The difference between the two German words is that only Christians have a *Beruf* (both calling to faith in Jesus and into an outer status),[99] while everyone has a *Stand* (noun: station). *Beruf* is a Christian's earthly or spiritual work.[100] But unlike our modern idea of occupation or paid work, Luther's definition of *Beruf* had multiple outer statuses: biological (father, mother, son, daughter, etc.), community (officeholder, church leader, etc.), and home (master, servant, husband, wife, etc.).[101] Those who were not

---

92. Heiges, *Christian's Calling*, 54.

93. Bennethum, *Listen*, 19.

94. Volf, *Work in the Spirit*, 156.

95. Kolden, "Luther on Vocation," 386.

96. Holl, "History of Word *Vocation*," 151.

97. Wingren, *Luther on Vocation*, ix; Douglas, "Talent and Vocation," 287; Holl, "History of Word *Vocation*," 152.

98. Placher, *Callings*, 7.

99. Heiges, *Christian's Calling*, 49.

100. Wingren, *Luther on Vocation*, 1–2.

101. Wingren, *Luther on Vocation*, 4–5; Heiges, *Christian's Calling*, 50–51.

Christian did not have a *Beruf*, for they lacked faith and thus were not pleasing to God. Luther's doctrine of vocation is inseparable from faith, for vocation is impossible without faith.[102] *Beruf* was not just *any* work; it was faithful obedience to God *in* work.[103] Vocation was transformational and defined a Christian's identity.[104] Luther completely reversed vocational theology: those isolated in monasteries did not have a calling; rather, God's calling is realized through work in the community.[105]

God's call (*Berufung*) is to a concrete, personal office (*Beruf*) where one serves as God's masks or voice.[106] Luther, being born as a private person, was not qualified to preach. He details this process in his John 8:12 sermon. Being a public person, with an office and the title of Doctor Martin Luther, had made him a preacher. "I am preaching at the request and behest of others. Otherwise let the devil do the preaching!"[107] The same process applies to Luther's office as a husband and father. "If someone were to come into my house and say, 'I am to be man of the house here,' I would tell him: 'No, brother, the Holy Spirit told me to be master in my house. . . . For I have God's command, which reads: 'This house and these servants are entrusted to your rule.' I am master here, and you know it."[108] A person is not born into an office but is called by their competence in service to the community.

One of Luther's key assertions that reversed church doctrine is that everyone who is baptized has a calling from God. All Christians bear the responsibility and opportunity to live in response to God's saving grace in Jesus Christ. Vocation encompasses the whole life of a Christian. It gives purpose and meaning to all activities and relationships.[109] The earthly response to God is directed

---

102. Badcock, *Way of Life*, 37.
103. Marshall, *Kind of Life*, 24.
104. Fink, "Liberating Those Who Work," 21.
105. Holl, "History of Word *Vocation*," 153.
106. Douglas, "Talent and Vocation," 290.
107. Luther, *Sermons on the Gospel* (LW 23), 342.
108. Luther, *Sermons on the Gospel* (LW 23), 322.
109. Bennethum, *Listen*, 41.

outward in service to humankind;[110] it is service to others in love.[111] This can be seen in Luther's sermon on Matt 7:12: "In everything do to others as you would have them do to you, for this is the law and the prophets." He uses examples from everyday life on how to treat your neighbor: workshop, needle or thimble, beer barrel, goods, and scales. He sees all people as preachers in their daily work. "Friend, use me in your relations with your neighbor just as you would want your neighbor to use his property in his relations with you."[112]

Luther uses the phrase "cross of vocation" to stipulate that loving service directed toward others, while benefiting the neighbor, comes at a cost. Bearing a cross may entail trivial tasks and/or great hardships, even death. It ranges from taking care of children to being sentenced to death for heresy during the Reformation. Vocation parallels the cross of Jesus Christ.[113] But the faithful are joyful in their vocation because the Holy Spirit is present and the love of God is active.[114] The character of a called person changes from being strictly of the flesh to Spirit filled.[115] God is working through a person's vocation. Luther's theology is dualistic. He sets humans between God and the devil. The called are bound by God and seek good works for their neighbor's sake through vocation, not for the sake of salvation. The unfaithful have no vocation and are bound to the devil.[116]

Luther strongly believed that he was commanded by God to be a pastor, and even though he was "weary and unhappy," he could not keep silent or cease teaching. "It is true that all Christians are priests, but not all are pastors. For to be a pastor one must be not only a Christian and a priest but must have an office and a field of work committed to him. This call and command make pastors and

---

110. Wingren, *Luther on Vocation*, 44–45.
111. Wingren, *Luther on Vocation*, 33; Heiges, *Christian's Calling*, 52–54.
112. Luther, *Sermon on the Mount* (*LW* 21), 237.
113. Wingren, *Luther on Vocation*, 29.
114. Wingren, *Luther on Vocation*, 44–45.
115. Wingren, *Luther on Vocation*, 67.
116. Wingren, *Luther on Vocation*, 105.

preachers."¹¹⁷ He cites Ps 51:17 ("The sacrifice acceptable to God is a broken spirit; a broken and contrite heart, O God, you will not despise") to support people accepting the calling God gives them rather than choosing it themselves. It is the devil that "disturbs every mind, in order that he may make void the calling of every person and to tempt him by seducing him to that for which he has not been called, as if God were a fool and did not know where He wished to call a person."¹¹⁸

Luther was a product of the culture of his time. Medieval society was stratified into social hierarchies, and there was little social mobility.¹¹⁹ Peasants remained peasants, and nobility remained nobility. Trades were passed down generation to generation. Luther was fortunate to have been educated, because otherwise, he would have remained in his father's mining business. However, Luther advocated that the social structures remain, primarily for two reasons: to maintain order and to keep people from taking monastic vows for salvation.¹²⁰ He was so focused on salvation by faith alone that he was blinded by rigid medieval order,¹²¹ a human-imposed practice antithetical to the kingdom of God. Luther believed in the omnipotence of God and that God had ordained the existing social structures. What God commands, humans must obey.¹²² Perhaps if Luther had lived to see the industrial age and modern and postmodern society, he would have altered his views.¹²³

Luther's gravest mistake, felt for centuries, was his exegesis of 1 Cor 7:20 where Luther uses *Beruf* for the Greek *klēsis*. In 1523, Luther published his *Commentaries on 1 Corinthians 7*.¹²⁴ He states that Paul tells the Corinthians in his first letter (7:20), that God's call of the gospel ("evangelical call") comes to them within their

---

117. Luther, *Selected Psalms 2* (*LW* 13), 65–66.
118. Luther, *Lectures on Romans* (*LW* 25), 338.
119. Troeltsch, *Social Teachings*, 1:296.
120. Bennethum, *Listen*, 60.
121. Heiges, *Christian's Calling*, 63–64.
122. Heiges, *Christian's Calling*, 57; Wingren, *Luther on Vocation*, 99.
123. Hardy, *Fabric of This World*, 64.
124. Luther, *Commentaries* (*LW* 28), 39–47.

current vocation. Humans are not to give up their *Stand* when God calls. They are to remain in their present position, *im Beruf*.[125] God wills people to remain in their vocation. Luther insists that free movement across societal stations, such as rulers being equal to peasants, would disrupt God's will, order, and authority. "Faith and the Christian life are so free in essence that they are bound to no particular order or estate of society, but they are to be found in and throughout all orders and estates."[126] Freedom of conscience is granted, but not freedom of station.[127] Rulers are not to preach the word, and ministers are not to rule. Luther acknowledges that "there are very few who live satisfied with their lot, . . . although there is no other way of serving God than to walk in simple faith and then stick diligently to one's calling and to keep a good conscience."[128] When German peasants demanded human rights and defied their landowners, the upper hierarchies crushed their disobedience. Luther states: "Remain in your station in life, be it high or low, and continue in your vocation. Beware of overreaching . . . Rather say, 'O God, heavenly father, defend me against haughtiness.'"[129] In his lectures on Gal 6:4 ("All must test their own work; then that work, rather than their neighbor's work, will become a cause for pride"), Luther states: "Someone who is a magistrate, a householder, a servant, a teacher, a pupil, etc., should remain in his calling and do his duty there, properly and faithfully, without concerning himself about what lies outside his own vocation."[130] Vocation and station both end at death, when all are equal in the kingdom of God.[131] Christians should, during their time on earth, joyfully and humbly accept their assigned *Stand*, be it lowly or lofty, and focus on serving others.[132] Striving for self-fulfillment diverts from

125. Wingren, *Luther on Vocation*, 64.
126. Luther, *Commentaries* (LW 28), 39.
127. Wingren, *Luther on Vocation*, 111.
128. Luther, *Lectures on Genesis* (LW 3), 128.
129. Wingren, *Luther on Vocation*, 130.
130. Luther, *Lectures on Galatians* (LW 27), 119.
131. Wingren, *Luther on Vocation*, 168.
132. Wingren, *Luther on Vocation*, 174–75.

Charismata

God's command to love our neighbors. Follow God's command by remaining in vocation.[133]

A few scholars have suggested that Luther was not opposed to social mobility but did oppose people joining religious organizations to please God.[134] I disagree. Luther desired order and his 1 Cor 7:20 exegesis gave him the ammunition to keep the existing society in place,[135] regardless of the biblical evidence against discriminating hierarchal structures. A complete 1 Cor 7 exegesis counters Luther's on 7:20, as discussed earlier.

Luther's argument for staying within a station runs counter to his own life (son of a miner, then law student, then monk, and finally a professor) and his views on gifts of the Holy Spirit. He did make exceptions for young people with scholastic talent; they could complete their education, via support from parents and governments, thus rising in social status through natural abilities.[136] Luther's one exception was most likely founded upon on his own rise through education, which runs counter to his *im Beruf* theology.

In his Large and Small Catechisms, Luther writes that the Holy Spirit both calls and gifts humans:

> called together (*zusammen-berufen*) by the Holy Ghost in one faith, one mind, and understanding, with manifold gifts[137]

> The Holy Ghost has called (*berufen*) me by the gospel, enlightened me with His gifts.[138]

Yet, a person born to peasant parents working as laborers under a landowner must remain there even though gifted with musical, linguistic, or mathematical skills. Citing 1 Cor 12:5–6, Luther

---

133. Wingren, *Luther on Vocation*, 227.
134. Bennethum, *Listen*, 52.
135. Placher, *Callings*, 207.
136. Heiges, *Christian's Calling*, 58–59.
137. Heiges, *Christian's Calling*, 47.
138. Heiges, *Christian's Calling*, 46.

inconsistently admits that "not all are competent in everything."[139] His stance of remaining in station is both illogical and a misuse of God's gifts. His theology of remaining in vocation is totally foreign to modern and postmodern cultures, which view vocation as an individual choice based on gifts, detached from economic or social settings.[140] Unfortunately, Luther's theological error carried through Protestant theology until the age of Enlightenment, thus constraining individual freedom and the effective use of God's gifts.

JOHN CALVIN (1509-64)

Martin Luther survived the Protestant Reformation and kept the fires of change burning. Other areas of Europe took up his torch and started their own fires. It was John Calvin who organized Protestant theology into systematic doctrines of the Christian faith that coherently challenged the Church of Rome's theology. Calvin grew up in France and was educated at the University of Paris, where he learned Latin. Like Luther, he studied law, first at the University of Orléans and later at the University of Bourges, where he learned Greek. Sometime during his studies, he shifted from his Church of Rome beliefs to Reformed theology. While in Paris, his Reformed views were noticed, and he fled to safer locations, eventually settling in Strasbourg and Geneva. While in Geneva (1538), he admitted to being called by God and did not shirk from God's command.[141]

Calvin was not only brilliant in his understanding of Scripture and classical Christian literature, but his legal training also gave precision and organization to his writings. In 1536, Calvin published his masterpiece, *Institutes of the Christian Religion*, an apologia (defense) of the Reformed faith. He revised and expanded *Institutes* until his death. Calvin lived a disciplined life

---

139. Luther, *Church and Ministry 2* (*LW* 40), 44.
140. Badcock, *Way of Life*, 44.
141. Douglas, "Talent and Vocation," 263.

and expected his congregation to follow suit. This led to several confrontations, one which led to his expulsion from Geneva in 1537. In 1541, he was called back to Geneva and lived there for the remainder of his life. He diligently wrote and preached full time, but somehow also found time to work with civic leaders on political and social projects. Calvin was a man of action.

Calvin is probably best known for his emphasis on predestination: God's eternal decree by which all creatures are foreordained to eternal life or death. The question arose: Who are elected by God for eternal life, and who are elected by God for death? Calvin did not worry about this issue, as those professing faith in Christ are the elect. Dr. Max Weber, a German professor of economics at the Universities of Freiburg and Heidelberg, published a groundbreaking book, *The Protestant Ethic and the Spirit of Capitalism*, in two parts, the first in 1904 and the second in 1905. He wrote subsequent remarks and rebuttals until his death in 1920. Weber's thesis was that election became a major issue in the years after Calvin's theological publications. "Indeed, the next life absolutely dominated people's religious thinking at that time. The moral awakening, which considerably influenced the *practical* life of believers, would *not* have been set in motion without the overarching power held by the next life over the believer."[142] No longer could a person feel certain of eternal life just by following the church's prescribed process.

Calvin believed that humans exist to serve the glorification of God. The predestined Christian exists "to increase God's glory in the world through the implementation of His commandments." God desires Christians to engage in community activities that transform society. Vocation is the mechanism to further God's transformational activity.[143] "*Work without rest in a vocational calling* was recommended as the best possible means to *acquire* the self-confidence that one belonged among the elect. Work, and work alone, banishes religious doubt and gives certainty of one's

---

142. Weber, *Protestant Ethic*, 115; emphasis original.
143. Weber, *Protestant Ethic*, 122.

status among the saved."[144] Calvin certainly believed that only faith achieved salvation and advocated a balanced life, not a life of just work. But his emphasis on predestination and faith alone left a void within the laity, who were accustomed to the Church of Rome's formulistic approach to salvation certainty. Protestant theology based on Scripture was tempting, but the public desired certainty. Weber's thesis was that productive work provided the proof. "Good works are indispensable as *signs* of election. They are technical means, but not ones that can be used to purchase salvation. Rather, good works serve to banish the anxiety surrounding the question of one's salvation."[145]

Luther and Calvin never met nor corresponded directly but were knowledgeable of each other and their respective theological positions. Both advocated that vocation was much more expansive than paid employment, that God equates all stations of life that serve the neighbor, and that a person should stay in their station and serve without complaint.[146] In the major vocational assumptions, Calvin's and Luther's positions were essentially the same.[147] Their differences were more related to emphasis. Luther's vocational theology centered on faith in God that produces spontaneous love towards the neighbor, while Calvin's vocational theology centered on the elect actively using their God-given gifts effectively. Vocation, for Luther, is the means by which God bestows gifts upon the faithful, while for Calvin, vocation is the means to give glory to God by using God's gifts productively. Luther was more concerned about transformational love and less concerned about getting things done; Calvin was a vocational activist who advocated producing results for the benefit of the community. Both agreed that all Christian skills stem from the operation of the Holy Spirit.[148] They agreed that the Holy Spirit first endowed people with gifts and the necessary qualifications before bestowing them

---

144. Weber, *Protestant Ethic*, 125; emphasis original.
145. Weber, *Protestant Ethic*, 127; emphasis original.
146. Stevens, *Doing God's Business*, 47.
147. Douglas, "Talent and Vocation," 292.
148. Volf, *Work in the Spirit*, 130; Calvin, *Institutes*, 167–68, 2.2.14–16.

with the office to serve the common good.¹⁴⁹ The Church in Rome promoted the contemplative life and demoted earthly tasks. Calvin elevated work as a required usage of God-given gifts; Luther was more passive and stood somewhere between the two.¹⁵⁰

Calvin's doctrine of vocation is concisely stated in his *Institutes*: "Every man's mode of life, therefore, is a kind of station assigned him by the Lord, that he may not be always driven about at random.... It is enough to know that in everything the call of the Lord is the foundation and beginning of right action. He who does not act with reference to it will never, in the discharge of duty, keep the right path." This statement parallels Luther's theology. Calvin supports Luther's "cross of vocation" by highlighting the "toils, annoyances, and other burdens" endured in vocation. However, "no work will be so mean and sordid as not to have a splendor and value in the eye of God."¹⁵¹ His more inclusive definition of vocation is like Luther's.

Luther and Calvin agreed on the exegesis of 1 Cor 7:20 that persons are to be satisfied with their own office and not envy others. "Be subject to the arrangement which God has appointed, that we may not, to no purpose, resist his will."¹⁵² However, Calvin was more flexible on social movement.

> Each should be content with his calling, and persist in it, and not be eager to change to something else.... But at this point someone is asking if Paul wishes to impose something binding on people, for what he says may seem to suggest that each one is tied to his calling, and must not give it up. But it would be asking far too much, if a tailor were not permitted to learn another trade, or a merchant to change to farming. To that I would reply that that is not the apostle's intention, for he only wishes to correct the thoughtless eagerness which impels some to change their situation without any proper reason.¹⁵³

149. Calvin, *Corinthians* (Pringle), 413–14.
150. Heiges, *Christian's Calling*, 60–63.
151. Calvin, *Institutes*, 472, 3.10.6.
152. Calvin, *Corinthians* (Pringle), 409–10.
153. Calvin, *Corinthians* (Fraser), 153.

Premodern (Creation to 1687)

A year before Calvin published *Institutes*, he wrote a preface to the New Testament in the Bible of Olivétan. In section 1, he states that in the Genesis fall story, man (humans) "was despoiled and divested of all his glory and alienated from all the gifts which were entrusted to him."[154] In Calvin's commentary on 1 Cor 12, the Holy Spirit distributes a variety of gifts and "orders every one to be contented with his own gifts, and cultivate the particular department that has been assigned to him."[155] But no one has enough gifts so as not to need help from others. The Holy Spirit distributes the gifts so that all "contribute to the common advantage." It is through diversity that "God unites us mutually to one another."[156]

His emphasis on the role of the Holy Spirit's gifts in the elect allowed for personal abilities to blossom. Calvin was more rational, as he favored higher productivity, which entailed social mobility.[157] Luther emphasized God's gifts discerned within a station, while Calvin emphasized the duty to use God's gifts for the sake of the neighbor. Calvin sought the best station to employ God's gifts[158] and to give proper order to the world.[159] Both agreed that vocational satisfaction, while a valuable attribute, is secondary to serving the neighbor.[160]

New terms and definitions were created as Reformed doctrine developed. *General* calling is God's pursuit of individuals to a life of faith in Jesus Christ. Over time, general calling was given many synonymous names: corporate, heavenly, holy, ordinary, original, principal, special, spiritual, and universal. These various names muddled and confused vocational terminology. Calvin, a strong advocate of preaching the word, defined general calling as the preached word invoking an individual to faith. *Special* calling is God's specific, direct, and undeniable call to individuals to

---

154. Neuser, "Calvin's Theology," 23.
155. Calvin, *Corinthians* (Pringle), 398.
156. Calvin, *Corinthians* (Pringle), 404.
157. Doriani, *Work*, 71–72.
158. Hardy, *Fabric of This World*, 66.
159. Stevens, *Doing God's Business*, 47–51.
160. Hardy, *Fabric of This World*, 98.

CHARISMATA

perform a task or mission. Calvin, a firm believer in predestination, classified special calling as working only in the elect to bring them to faith.[161]

Calvin's exegesis on the parable of the talents (Matt 25:14–30) is a classic example of him reshaping the meaning of the word "talents." Calvin interpreted v. 15 ("to each according to his ability") as "Christ does not distinguish between natural gifts and the gifts of the Spirit; for we have neither power nor skill which ought not to be acknowledged as having been received from God. ... It is because God, as he has assigned to everyone his place, and has bestowed on him natural gifts."[162] Prior to Calvin, talents were defined as spiritual gifts that God gave to Christians. Calvin revolutionized and expanded the definition of talents "in terms of one's calling,"[163] to be found within a person and "given to us for God's pleasure and the neighbor's good."[164] His interpretation led to our modern definition of the word "talent." In his very first chapter of *Institutes*, Calvin writes: "It is perfectly obvious, that the endowments [talents] which we possess cannot possibly be from ourselves; no, that our very being is nothing else than subsistence in God alone."[165] Knowing God and knowing yourself are mutually connected. Christians do not choose their talents, as talents comes from God, but Christians are commanded by God to dedicate their talents in vocational service towards their neighbors and to the glory of God.

After Calvin's death, Calvinism spread through various Swiss cantons, the Netherlands, parts of France, and Scotland. It conflicted with the Church of England, the aftermath of Henry VIII's succession from the Church of Rome. Calvin's desire for discipline, productivity, and order were rigorously applied. Personal dress was plain, functional, and dark. Conduct was strict, dour, and regulated. Church buildings were stripped bare, services were

---

161. Placher, *Callings*, 232; Calvin, *Institutes*, 643, 3.24.8.
162. Calvin, *Harmony of the Evangelists*, 442.
163. Marshall, *Kind of Life*, 25.
164. Banks and Stevens, *Everyday Christianity*, 1001.
165. Calvin, *Institutes*, 4, 1.1.1.

lengthy, and the preached word was steeped in theology. During the week, diligent and productive work was praised, along with thrift. It was the Puritans who maximized Calvinism and changed the definition of vocation.

PURITANS

Puritans were members of the Church of England who sought to purify the church by returning it to Scripture. They aligned theologically and ascetically with Calvinism.[166] Anglicans were defenders of the traditional practices of the Church of England. They were, in general, "more Catholic" than Puritans although Anglicans had separated from the Church in Rome. This terminology is generalized, as both Christian groups were committed members of the Church of England. Even in the postmodern Church of England, parish churches generally lean either to Puritan or Anglican mannerisms.

Dr. Paul Marshall, professor of political theory at the Institute for Christian Studies in Toronto, charts in his book *A Kind of Life Imposed on Man* the transformation of vocation from the Elizabethan Age (1558–1603) to the early Enlightenment Age (end of the seventeenth century). It was during this period that the Protestant theology of vocation, as articulated by Luther and Calvin, transitioned into our modern vocabulary. I will give a brief overview primarily founded upon Marshall's more detailed analysis.

William Tyndale (1494–1536), an Oxford-educated linguist, was the first to translate the Hebrew and Greek Scriptures into English. For this and his Reformed theological beliefs, he died as a heretic. Tyndale's views on vocation aligned with Luther and Calvin: Christians must accept their current estate and not change to another.[167] Thus, at the very onset of the English Reformation, Luther and Calvin's vocational theology was adopted. Early Protestant Reformers, such as Robert Crowley (1517–88), Thomas

---

166. González, *Story of Christianity*, 2:194.
167. Marshall, *Kind of Life*, 31.

Beacon (1512–67), and John Hooper (1495–1555), were consistent in their beliefs that a Christian's general calling occurred by being a member of society and, once called, Christians were to remain in their assigned station. A small difference, noted by Marshall, was that the English viewed calling "as something immanent in society rather than as a call to specific duties which come to one in a social position."[168]

It was William Perkins (1558–1602), a Cambridge fellow and theologian, who solidified vocational theology in *A Treatise of the Vocations*, first published in 1605 after his death. His original twenty-nine-page treatise was a classical Reformational manuscript full of legalistic doctrine. Perkins begins his treaty with a general definition: "A vocation or calling is a certain kind of life, ordained and imposed on man by God, for the common good."[169] The omnipotent God designates, through election, a "certain kind of life." Perkins then formulates two general rules: first, "whatever any man attempts or does, either in word or deed, he must do it by virtue of his calling; and he must keep himself within the compass, limits, or precincts of it"; and second, "every man must do the duties of his calling with diligence."[170] Perkins clearly embraces Calvinism when he defines idleness and slothfulness as "two damnable sins."[171] Richard Baxter (1615–91), English church leader and Puritan theologian, was a prolific writer and published *Christian Directory* in 1673. Weber states that Baxter's book "is the most comprehensive compendium of Puritan moral theology."[172] Baxter agreed with Perkins and wrote that idleness threatened the soul more than wealth. The cure for idleness was hard work.[173] Moderate recreation and disablement, in addition to

---

168. Marshall, *Kind of Life*, 32–35.
169. Perkins, "Treatise of the Vocations," 6.
170. Perkins, "Treatise of the Vocations," 8.
171. Perkins, "Treatise of the Vocations," 9.
172. Weber, *Protestant Ethic*, 159.
173. Barnes, *Redeeming Capitalism*, 63–64.

weekly Sabbath, were allowed.[174] Every able person was required to perform hard work.

Hard, disciplined work and frugal living led to wealth creation. Calvin did not believe that the accumulation of wealth, per se, was a problem. Puritans condemned pursuing money and accumulating material goods without end. What was "morally reprehensible" was "*resting* upon one's possessions and the *enjoyment* of wealth."[175] Only *activity* that serves the community gives glory to God. "Of all the sins, the *wasting of time* constitutes the first and, in principle, the most serious." A person has only a certain amount of earthly time to "make firm" their election. Baxter equates vocational idleness to godlessness.[176] This Puritan morality goes completely against postmodern societal norms.

Perkins subdivided calling into two types. The first, general, "is that calling whereby a man is called out of the world to be a child of God, a member of Christ, and an heir of the kingdom of heaven."[177] This aligns with New Testament Scripture. The second, personal, "is the execution of some particular office arising from that distinction which God makes between man and man in every society."[178] General always takes precedence over personal.[179] He acknowledges "inward gifts which God bestows on every man" based on 1 Cor 12 and "order" where "God has appointed that in every society, one person should be above or under another."[180] The stratification of society into hierarchies was God's design to maintain order within society.

Perkins proceeds with five general rules for personal callings. For example, "every man must judge that the particular calling in which God has placed him, is the best of all callings for him." Christians are to be content within their own standing and not "think

---

174. Perkins, "Treatise of the Vocations," 44.
175. Weber, *Protestant Ethic*, 159; emphasis original.
176. Weber, *Protestant Ethic*, 160; emphasis original.
177. Perkins, "Treatise of the Vocations," 9.
178. Perkins, "Treatise of the Vocations," 12.
179. Perkins, "Treatise of the Vocations," 17.
180. Perkins, "Treatise of the Vocations," 13.

other men's callings are better for us than our own."[181] Perkins dives deeper and deeper into theological legalism. It is interesting to note that personal callings are divided into "two sorts." The first sort is "of the *essence and foundation* of any society." Occupations, such as magistrates and ministers, are considered essential since "without which the society cannot exist." The second sort, such as physicians and lawyers, "serve only for the good, happy, and *quiet estate* of a society."[182] While all personal callings are equal, it seems that some are more equal than others.[183]

But how does a person choose a calling that God has given? First, "we are to choose honest and lawful callings to walk in." Second, men are to choose based on "affection" and "gifts," then seek advice and help from others.[184] Parents are to choose for their children based on the child's "inclination" and "natural gifts."[185] And third, "he that is fit for various callings, must make a choice of the best." These rules give some leeway in a choice of calling, which allows for social movement, and aligns with Luther's vocational theology. Perkins shows his personal bias when he states: "Academic callings must have the first place."[186] But how does a person have certainty that what they choose as a personal calling is what God desires? This question would haunt Protestants for centuries. According to Perkins, vocation seems to be both imposed by God but also chosen according to one's gifts. Baxter follows Perkins's dualism: "Choose that employment or calling (so far as you have your choice) in which you may be most serviceable to God." He leans more to personal gifts with children: "You must consider, not only the *Will* of the *Child* or the *Parents* but the natural fitness of their body and mind."[187]

---

181. Perkins, "Treatise of the Vocations," 14.
182. Perkins, "Treatise of the Vocations," 17; emphasis original.
183. Marshall, *Kind of Life*, 45.
184. Perkins, "Treatise of the Vocations," 18.
185. Perkins, "Treatise of the Vocations," 19.
186. Perkins, "Treatise of the Vocations," 20.
187. Douglas, "Talent and Vocation," 296–97; emphasis original.

PREMODERN (CREATION TO 1687)

After Elizabeth I died, she was succeeded by James VI of Scotland (King James I of England) who ruled from 1603 until 1625. His reign brought increased conflicts between Protestants and Catholics. The subsequent reign of Charles I (ruled 1625-49) ushered in even more conflicts between Puritans in Parliament and a powerful monarch who aligned closely with Catholics. This led to the English Civil War (1642-51) and the 1649 beheading of Charles I. It was during this post-Elizabethan period that vocation theology began to separate from strictly theological definitions into secular definitions. "Callings were understood more in the sense of employments. The words 'trade,' 'employment,' 'occupation,' 'calling,' and 'vocation' became interchangeable.[188] ... The normative guidelines for work tended to flow less and less from the particular commands of God and more and more from the particular duties and roles which were current in the society."[189]

By the mid-seventeenth century, the term "secular work" appeared in literature. Thomas Watson (1620-86), an English Puritan preacher, states, "You have done all your secular work on the six days, you should now cease from the labor of your calling, and dedicate the seventh day to the Lord."[190] After the English Civil War and the return of the monarchy to King Charles II (ruled 1660-85), a Christian's calling, except for ministers, meant having an occupation. A split occurred in Luther's vocation theology.[191] God's general call to faith in Jesus Christ remained theological. Personal calling became secularized.[192] Even the rigid social structures founded upon 1 Cor 7:20 started to be discarded as not compatible with the growing industrialization.[193] John Goodwin (c. 1594-1665), English preacher and theologian, states that, when necessary, "one could violate the law of callings: 'callings

---

188. Marshall, *Kind of Life*, 45.
189. Marshall, *Kind of Life*, 46.
190. Marshall, *Kind of Life*, 48.
191. Marshall, *Kind of Life*, 49.
192. Stevens, *Doing God's Business*, 49; Guinness, *Call*, 39.
193. Marshall, *Kind of Life*, 50.

were made for men, and not men for callings."[194] Puritan vocation doctrine now echoed Jesus's statement about the Sabbath (Mark 2:27). There was even a slight shift from calling to gifts. Stephen Charnock (1628–80), English Puritan minister, writes: "So among men there are several inclinations and several abilities, as donations from God, for the common advantage of human society . . . one man is qualified for one employment, another marked out by God for a different work."[195] Matthew Poole (1624–79), an English Nonconformist and biblical commentator, did not adhere to Luther's strict interpretation of 1 Cor 7:20. "They too far strain this text who interpret it into an obligation upon all men, not to alter that particular way or course of life and trading to which they were educated, or in which they formally had been engaged. . . . Such a change was allowed because the world and occupations were seen to be so changeable. . . . A child is now designed for this, then for that—How strangely are things wheeled about by providence."[196] By the Restoration, the static interpretation of 1 Cor 7:20 was "comparatively rare."[197]

Calling as the express command of God slowly began to change into a natural right. René Descartes (1596–1650), in his publication of *Discourse on the Method* in 1637, declared, *Cogito, ergo sum* (I think, therefore I am). Descartes and other philosophers, rooted in human reasoning, influenced Christianity. Once unthinkable, the existence of God was challenged through reason. "It became possible to speak of callings without speaking of God, or indeed of any caller whatsoever. The calling was now abstract right and duty."[198] Luther and Calvin had brought spiritual meaning to all vocations after the medieval church had limited it to the spiritual professionals. By the late-seventeenth century, philosophers and diligent English industrialists assigned vocation back to

---

194. Marshall, *Kind of Life*, 77.
195. Hardy, *Fabric of This World*, 61.
196. Marshall, *Kind of Life*, 49–50.
197. Marshall, *Kind of Life*, 70.
198. Marshall, *Kind of Life*, 84.

the church professions. Calling was again reserved for professional ministry within a church.[199]

Calvinism maintained that idleness was sinful, and hard work, outside of the Sabbath, was normative, although Calvin did advocate a balanced life. He was against the Church of Rome that advocated asceticism, since God provided generous gifts to humans yet placed limits by denouncing materialism and wasteful practices. It was the Puritans who took Calvin's theology and placed it into overdrive, something Calvin would not have supported.

Weber highlights two themes on Baxter's treatise on Christian vocation: "First, work is the tried and proven *means* for the practice of *asceticism*."[200] The more time spent working, the less time is spent on materialism. Both Luther and Calvin were fervently against the monastic beliefs that advocated self-denial to achieve salvation. It is shocking that within a hundred years of the Protestant Reformation, Puritans reintroduced asceticism. Instead of placing spiritualism above the secular occupations, as the Church of Rome advocated, the Puritans made work sacred.

"Second, in addition and above all, as ordained by God, the purpose of life *itself* involves work. . . . An unwillingness to work is a sign that one is not among the saved."[201] How does a Protestant seek the certainty of salvation? By the fruits of their work: "its economic profitability."[202] How do Puritans rectify their vocation theology that accumulating wealth is a sin and economic profitability is a sign of salvation? Puritans juggle their dualistic theology through the lens of telos. If the devout become lazy and enjoy their accumulated wealth, then it is sinful to build wealth. A carefree life of enjoyment goes against a Puritan's calling. However, if a Puritan works diligently within their vocational calling, then striving for wealth "is not only morally permitted but expected."[203]

---

199. Stevens, *Doing God's Business*, 50–51.
200. Weber, *Protestant Ethic*, 160; emphasis original.
201. Weber, *Protestant Ethic*, 161; emphasis original.
202. Weber, *Protestant Ethic*, 163.
203. Weber, *Protestant Ethic*, 164.

Charismata

On November 11, 1620, Puritans landed at Provincetown Harbor, Cape Cod (Massachusetts). A year later, having survived the winter, the Puritans gathered to celebrate a Thanksgiving harvest meal. These early English settlers, along with other immigrants, continued to grow and prosper in the new world. By the eighteenth century, colonies were established along the East Coast of the soon-to-be United States of America.

Modern (1687 to 1900)

THE SPIRIT OF CAPITALISM

Protestantism was the dominant religion in colonial America, and Calvinism was the major cultural influence. The new world was fertile and teeming with rich resources. All that was required was human and financial capital. Europeans seeking fortune and freedom immigrated across the Atlantic. The age of Enlightenment (1715–89) ushered in the start of the modern period, during which human reasoning began to question Christian doctrines. Puritan vocational theology gradually moved from its theological roots into the growing capitalistic economy, directly opposite to the economically simplistic medieval traditionalism.

Before the American Revolutionary War (1775–83), this transition was well underway. Benjamin Franklin (1706–90) was an influential person who paved the way. While he had been raised in a Calvinist home, Franklin was an enlightened man guided by reason and not Protestant doctrine. All of Franklin's moral admonishments are applied in a utilitarian fashion:

> Honesty is *useful* because it leads to the availability of credit. Punctuality, industry, and frugality are also useful and are *therefore* virtues. It would follow from this that, for example, the *appearance* of honesty, wherever it accomplishes the same end, would suffice. Moreover, in Franklin's eyes an unnecessary surplus of this virtue must be seen as unproductive wastefulness. Indeed, whoever reads in his autobiography the story of his "conversion" to these virtues, or the complete discussions on

the usefulness of a strict preservation of the *appearance* of modesty and the intentional minimizing of one's own accomplishments in order to attain a general approval, will necessarily come to the conclusion that all virtues, according to Franklin, become virtues *only to the extent that they are useful to the individual*.[1]

Puritan vocational values, supported by Calvinism, migrated into a secular utilitarian organization of life. Franklin's truisms like "Time is money" and "A penny saved is a penny earned" established the spirit of capitalism as a cultural North American norm. What postmodern Americans take for granted in their capitalistic society began before the American Revolution with Puritan vocational theology, which then filtered into secular society.

The interesting aspect of the spirit of capitalism is its separation of work and pleasure. Weber, during the early twentieth century, stated:

> The complexity of this issue is above all apparent in the *summum bonum* [supreme good] of this "ethic": namely, the acquisition of money, and more and more money, takes place here simultaneously with the strictest avoidance of all spontaneous enjoyment of it. The pursuit of riches is fully stripped of all pleasurable, and surely all hedonistic, aspects.[2]

The Middle Ages exalted the sacred ascetic life. In less than three hundred years, the Protestant ethic ushered in the spirit of capitalism, which exalted the secular ascetic life. What the medieval church viewed "as an expression of filthy greed and a completely undignified character"[3] was now viewed in the modern period as a "manifestation of competence and proficiency in a *vocational calling*."[4] What was originally established theologically became anti-religious. Many modern capitalists, saturated with the spirit of capitalism, were either indifferent or openly hostile

---

1. Weber, *Protestant Ethic*, 79–80; emphasis original.
2. Weber, *Protestant Ethic*, 80.
3. Weber, *Protestant Ethic*, 82.
4. Weber, *Protestant Ethic*, 81; emphasis original.

Modern (1687 to 1900)

to religion. In a postmodern world, Weber's writings of over one hundred years ago still reverberate and cause one to ponder again: Why do "people live for their business rather than the reverse"?[5]

The age of Enlightenment progressed into the industrial age, a period of scientific discoveries, large-scale manufacturing, and labor abuses. People migrated from rural to urban locations seeking work as the population expanded. Education was broadened by public school funding. As the United States expanded westward, seminary-educated clergy were in short supply, so many Protestant denominations ordained spirit-filled lay persons to lead rural churches. The Second (1790–1850) and Third Great Awakenings (1850–1900) ushered in charismatic revivals and social movements such as temperance, abolition, and civil rights. The belief was that with education for all, enough government funding, and religious values, humanity would eventually obtain the kingdom of God. Human reasoning will prevail! Then came two world wars.

---

5. Weber, *Protestant Ethic*, 92.

Postmodern (1900 to Present)

KARL BARTH (1886-1968)

Karl Barth was born into an academic and pastoral Swiss family during a relatively peaceful period full of optimism, towards the end of the modern period. He was taught by the liberal theologian Adolf von Harnack (1851–1930), who questioned early church doctrine, promoted the social gospel, and traced the influences of Hellenistic philosophy in Scripture. Liberal theology was the mainstream within the Reformed Church at the start of the postmodern period.

During World War I, Barth was a pastor in Safenwil, Switzerland, and wrote *The Epistle to the Romans*. He broke with his liberal teachers and developed dialectical theology, also called crisis or neo-orthodox theology, which stressed the paradoxical nature of divine truth. He stood up to Nazism and was primarily responsible for writing the Barmen Declaration, which he personally mailed to Adolf Hitler. Barth was forced to resign his German professorship at the University of Bonn in 1935 and returned to his native Switzerland, where he taught until his retirement.

Barth was a prolific writer. His magnum opus, *Church Dogmatics*, contains over nine thousand pages of systematic theology. He was brilliant, but his lengthy and repetitive writings fog his theological concepts and make his work inaccessible to most Christians. He wrote about vocation late in his life in *The Doctrine of Creation*, ch. 12: "The Command of God the Creator."

Postmodern (1900 to Present)

Barth's vocation theology returned to its Calvinist roots and harkened back to the original definition of vocation as the calling of God: the divine summons. "The command of God is what claims man, not his work, or his lovable or unlovable fellows, or history, or the cosmos."[1] Recognizing his vocational roots is crucial for understanding Barth. God encounters individual men and women through God's revelation. Humans know God, not through their reason, but by God calling them to faith and obedience.[2] Vocation begins when an individual recognizes God's call and command. Barth reconfirms that vocation is far greater than simply a call to work. "He [a human] will always live in widely different spheres if he receives the divine calling and is obedient to it."[3] He stresses that the first vocation criterion is the responsibility to live by the commands of God, the caller. "The place of his responsibility, i.e., his vocation, is for every man a special calling."[4]

The second criterion is that every person live within his or her special historical situation, an external vocational limitation. A person cannot choose their historical situation, such as family, class, education, and environment, but a person can choose not to follow this path within their vocation. "He is not caged in it or chained to it. His situation is not his grave; it is rather his cradle."[5] Although the historical situation is created by others when a person is born, a person is not destined to follow this path within their vocation. Humans bear responsibility for their vocation and should not allow their historical situation to dominate their choices.

The third criterion lies within the person: their personal aptitude or God-given gifts. We can all relate to our own internal limitations and gifts. Yet, God still calls humans. "Within its limit, but also in its fulness, he stands before God and has to listen and answer and obey. He did not choose it. He was not asked whether

---

1. Barth, *Doctrine of Creation*, 587.
2. Badcock, *Way of Life*, 58.
3. Barth, *Doctrine of Creation*, 599.
4. Barth, *Doctrine of Creation*, 600.
5. Barth, *Doctrine of Creation*, 622.

CHARISMATA

he is pleased with it. He has received it from God, his Creator and Lord, as he enters upon decision and act."[6] Should a person worry that their internal limitations are not good enough? What if a person cannot perform their occupation as well as others can? Barth clearly says no and references 1 Cor 12 (variety of spiritual gifts) and Matt 25:14–30 (the parable of the talents)[7] as God instructing humans to use their God-given gifts to the best of their individual abilities. Barth does not use the terms "self-realization" or "self-fulfillment" in the use of human gifts and has been criticized for concentrating heavily on the divine call and obedience.[8] Barth shifted away from liberal theology that relied primarily on human reason, just as Luther shifted away from the Church of Rome's monasticism and the requirement of works to achieve salvation.

The fourth and last limitation on God's calling is every person has a sphere of operation within which to contribute to society. The calling that comes from God is not an accident, but humans have freedom in choosing. "The critical question is whether he [or she] will achieve the freedom of obedience in this particular sphere and under all the other signs of his creaturely vocation."[9] Humans fulfill the will of God within their independence and responsible choices. Barth concludes his four criteria and states that humans have to ask "at least three practical questions: first, of course, the question of correct or obedient choice of his sphere of operation; then of correct or obedient existence in the chosen sphere; and finally of the possibility of commanded and therefore correct or obedient change or transition from one sphere to another."[10]

Barth becomes practical again by examining what an individual should do when confronting several opportunities. Do Christians look inwardly towards their God-given gifts or externally when community beckons? Barth responds dialectically: "The correct decision is always made precisely where the two lines

---

6. Barth, *Doctrine of Creation*, 624.
7. Barth, *Doctrine of Creation*, 627–8.
8. Badcock, *Way of Life*, 57.
9. Barth, *Doctrine of Creation*, 632.
10. Barth, *Doctrine of Creation*, 634.

intersect."[11] Life is full of paradoxes and complexities! God's command is not as simple as humans would prefer, but multifaceted. Christians must consider both internal and external dimensions.[12] "God alone can give both the outward and the inward voice authority and compulsion. We must not fail to hear these two voices."[13] By listening to God, and to people God uses, a person will make the right choice in obedience to God's command. Barth advocates action rather than continual contemplation.[14] "A man can really learn to know his sphere of operation only as he occupies it and sets to work in it."[15] Barth, like Calvin, advocates performing vocation "to the best of my ability, skill, and conscience." He labels vocation a mystery where subject and object, humans and tasks, abilities, and willingness all meet. This is a situation where a person can choose to be genuinely faithful and obedient to God's call or guilty of "laziness, arbitrariness, and folly."[16] Barth chose obedience to God's call and command.

Barth tackles 1 Cor 7:20, abiding in the condition in which a person is called, head-on:

> It certainly means that he must not glance aside at the callings of others. It certainly means that he must apply himself wholeheartedly to his own. It certainly means, therefore, that he must not allow this application to be challenged or disturbed by the thought of other desirable or very different callings. There is no other calling for any man. Each has his own calling.[17]

Barth breaks with Luther's interpretation of 1 Cor 7:20: "There can be no doubt that we cannot accept his [Luther's] doctrine of vocation in the form thus far disclosed in his writings."[18]

11. Barth, *Doctrine of Creation*, 636.
12. Schuurman, *Vocation*, 159.
13. Barth, *Doctrine of Creation*, 636.
14. Hardy, *Fabric of This World*, 87–88.
15. Barth, *Doctrine of Creation*, 637.
16. Barth, *Doctrine of Creation*, 642–43.
17. Barth, *Doctrine of Creation*, 645–46.
18. Barth, *Doctrine of Creation*, 645.

He affirms that Christians can pursue other tasks or spheres of operation. What must remain is the calling, not the sphere of operation. Remaining in the calling means being open and ready to be called elsewhere. Did God err when a person was led in one direction, then changes? *No*, states Barth, as only humans err, not God. Perhaps God led a person in one direction to discover some new direction. Christians must be open to change within their calling. He also disagrees with Luther's placement of calling within a social order, as it places humans under a law based on history. The generations before Barth took the social order for granted and then assumed this was a divine imperative. Is this any different than being placed in a cloister because a person decided to be a priest?[19] "What right have we to exclude the possibility that the divine calling and man's corresponding obedience might one day transfer him altogether from his present sphere to another?"[20]

Changes can happen that are out of a person's control. One can work for a company and be reassigned to a new location or position. A pastor can be transferred by a bishop to a new congregation with different pastoral needs. A business closes and one seeks new employment. Sickness or age may cause radical changes. All these changes are still within the same calling. Spheres of operation change, but a Christian's calling remains. The more serious the change, the more individuals must ask themselves, is this "really the calling of God and not just our own caprice that we think we must follow."[21]

JACQUES ELLUL (1912-94)

Born a generation after Karl Barth, Dr. Jacques Ellul was a French philosopher, sociologist, ethicist, and lay theologian. He was a professor of history and sociology at the University of Bordeaux (France). Like Barth, he witnessed firsthand the evil of Nazism.

---

19. Marshall, *Kind of Life*, 69; Schuurman, *Vocation*, 28.
20. Barth, *Doctrine of Creation*, 645.
21. Barth, *Doctrine of Creation*, 646–47.

POSTMODERN (1900 TO PRESENT)

He participated in the French resistance during World War II and was decorated for rescuing French Jews from a near-certain death in concentration camps. He was well versed in the writings of Karl Barth and considered him the greatest twentieth-century theologian, though his admiration did not stop him from theological disagreements.

Both men believed that human reason cannot lead humans to God; it is God who reveals. Barth gives work a low priority, something necessary to sustain life, but on the periphery. Yet, as previously discussed, Barth sees vocation as a place of responsibility, and work is certainly included within a Christian's sphere of operation. Ellul was particularly knowledgeable of how Scripture defines vocation and how Christians link this with work. He advocates retaining the biblical terminology and its historical identity as discussed in the previous Scripture sections: "It is not necessary to undertake a lengthy study to realize that nothing in the Bible allows us to identify *work* with *calling*.... For if work was conceived as a calling, a vocation coming from God, the Bible would have accorded it an importance that it may not have had culturally."[22]

Ellul states that the linkage of work and calling was derived from two perspectives. First, Greek philosophy advocated a passion for unity, which influenced early Christianity. "The ideal life is '*One*,' undivided."[23] Work is a large part of human life and should not be separated from faith. And second, work allows humans to survive, and God wishes creation to thrive and prosper. During the Middle Ages, theologians devised theological dogma to give more universal directions on what kind of work pleased God. During the Reformation and into the modern period, work was elevated to such an extent that it was linked to the meaning of life. General calling cascaded down to a particular calling, in which individuals remained in their social station and sought God's direction for their personal vocation. Work became a means of individual redemption, as Weber notes. Eventually, vocation was secularized except for church professionals. Karl Marx (1818–83), an atheist,

22. Ellul, "Work and Calling," 8; Placher, *Callings*, 328; emphasis original.
23. Ellul, "Work and Calling," 9; emphasis original.

"lifts the ideology of work to its summit. Man is what he does (in his work). Work is what distinguishes man from the rest of nature, so he awards work an exceptional place and virtue."[24] Vocation started as a call from God to faithful obedience and transitioned into the secular virtue of work.

Capitalism has reduced work to a commodity, which breaks all theological connections to vocation.[25] In a technological society, "one cannot accept a man endowed with vocation, or God's calling,"[26] because humans are just following the laws of nature. Ellul uses the word "incarnate" (to embody) as a way that people express vocation. "Vocation tends to remain something purely inward, purely spiritual. Yet for a faith centered on the Incarnation, this is simply not acceptable."[27] The work that society offers contains no significance or satisfaction. Calling finds no possibilities of incarnation. Ellul believed that in his postmodern life, humans were powerless. He dismisses any profession that defends the poor (i.e., a doctor or lawyer) as "the victim of an illusion."[28] Surprisingly, Ellul offers volunteer work, such as his Prevention Club, as an example of genuine work, because it is "a large autonomy of action, unceasing innovation, and free choice."[29] Ellul was a Christian anarchist who didn't believe in governmental authority. The only authority for Christians is God's authority as embodied in the teachings of Jesus, especially within the Sermon on the Mount. His rationale for genuine work, such as his volunteer activities, is juxtaposed to his insignificant work, his university professorship; the difference lies in unstructured versus structured activities. Ellul advocates for complete vocational freedom for it to be significant. He doesn't accept any authority other than a supreme being. His vocational world would be chaos if implemented.

---

24. Ellul, "Work and Calling," 10.
25. Schuurman, *Vocation*, 83.
26. Ellul, "Work and Calling," 11.
27. Ellul, "Work and Calling," 12.
28. Ellul, "Work and Calling," 13.
29. Ellul, "Work and Calling," 15.

Ellul makes several dialectic arguments that counter his devaluing of work. First, through work, humans recognize their finitude and sinfulness before God. Second, work is incapable of giving meaning to life or uncovering ultimate truths. If work does produce joy, it is a gift from God that allows humans to give thanks. And third, work allows humanity to survive, hoping for a better future. The day of judgment has not arrived. Thus, humans are called to survive during their short period on earth and trust God in the absolute. Ellul advocates a Christian calling in an activity that modifies the world, "an activity that can only be gratuitous, while preserving the characteristics we usually attribute to work: seriousness, competence, continuity, invention. It seems to me [Ellul] that it is in this manner that activity can express vocation, calling, for the Christian."[30] Each person must choose their form of vocational incarnation. Instead of being called by God to a particular calling, Ellul believed that humans are called into a *disorder* established by humans. Vocation is questioning this human disorder and upsetting it.[31]

What is particularly absent from Ellul's writings on vocation is God giving humans skills to serve their neighbors, as expressed in the apostle Paul's writings on the gifts of the Spirit. Why aren't Ellul's gifts as a university teacher transforming his students to work for the kingdom? Ellul leaves unstated the process that humans must take to redeem postmodern work, yet his professorship can be a small vehicle for transformational change. He basically gave up on redeeming a capitalistic society. Luther advocates redeeming society through vocation, and Ellul accepts the status quo of a fallen society. Luther's vocational model is based upon a rigid hierarchical social system, and Ellul desired a disorderly, unstructured social system.[32] In reality, dialectic truth lies in both Luther and Ellul: we live in a broken world built on unjust systems, yet Christians are called to serve their neighbors and work towards the kingdom.

30. Ellul, "Work and Calling," 14.
31. Ellul, "Work and Calling," 16.
32. Hardy, *Fabric of This World*, 104–5.

CHARISMATA

MIROSLAV VOLF (BORN 1956)

The focus on the kingdom was forefront in the theological writings of Dr. Jürgen Moltmann (born 1926), retired professor of systematic theology at the University of Tübingen. His expertise was eschatology, the study of things to come. One of his doctoral students was Dr. Miroslav Volf, a Croatian theologian who is the Henry B. Wright Professor of Theology and Director of the Yale Center for Faith and Culture at Yale University. His dissertation was a theological evaluation of Karl Marx's (1818–83) understanding of work. He became dissatisfied with Protestant vocational theology as articulated during the Reformation and shifted to a *pneumatological* theology of work based on *charisma* (spiritual gifts). After publishing a series of theological journal papers on pneumatology,[33] he published *Work in the Spirit* in 1990. Volf tilted Protestant vocational theology from call to gifts.

In my book *Trading with God*, I wrote a chapter on Volf's doctrine of work. I will now focus on his pneumatological theology as it relates to vocation. Volf starts with the New Testament definition of calling (*klēsis*) as God's pursuit of individuals to a life of faith in Jesus Christ. This is referred to as a general or spiritual calling. The Reformers cascaded general calling to a particular or external calling,[34] God's call to a specific occupation or service as derived from 1 Cor 28–31. The appointed offices are related to services within the church. Volf agrees with general calling but employs "charisma" as the technical term for these tasks. "For charisma implies both *endowment* with a gift and the *call* of God to exercise this gift in a particular way for the benefit of the community. There is no charisma without call.... There is no genuine call without an endowment by the Spirit."[35] Volf defines vocation as "call-and-gift," founded upon New Testament ecclesiology and, by extension, applies his definition to secular occupations and services. Eschatology is now the primary source since the focus of gifts is

---

33. Volf, *Work in the Spirit*, vii–viii.
34. Volf, *Work in the Spirit*, 105–6.
35 Volf, *Work in the Spirit*, 132; emphasis original.

Postmodern (1900 to Present)

the kingdom.[36] The extension is based on logical reasoning. Does an accountant who works for an accounting firm and volunteers his or her accounting gifts at a church suddenly switch between secular and spiritual gifts? Did Martin Luther King Jr. preach at his church using his spiritual gifts only to switch to secular gifts when he gave his "Dream" speech on the Washington, DC, mall? "It is the same Spirit, given to Christians as the first installment of what is to come, that prompts them to do both secular and ecclesiastical work."[37] The Holy Spirit is at work in all gifts that serve the community.

Luther believed that only Christians have *Beruf* (calling both to faith in Jesus and to an outer status).[38] Those with *Beruf* are doing God's work; all others are doing the devil's work. Volf's charism theology has God's gifts given to *non-Christians* by analogy. "To the extent that non-Christians are open to the prompting of the Spirit, their work, too, is the cooperation with God in anticipation of the eschatological transformation of the world, even though they may not be aware of it."[39] Again, Volt deploys logic in his theology. If charisms, Volf's term for the Greek plural *charismata*, are used to assist destitute Christians, then do they cease when benevolences are given to non-Christians? "All functions of the fellowship ... are the result of the operation of the Spirit of God and are thus charismatic. The place of operation does not define charisms, but the manifestation of the Spirit for the divinely ordained purpose." Based on Pauline theology, he advocates that charisms be generic for all gifts, from the ordinary to the miraculous.[40]

Volf agrees with most modern theologians that Luther misinterpreted 1 Cor 7:20. "It does not designate a calling peculiar to every Christian and distinguishing one Christian from another.... It refers to the quality of life that should characterize *all Christians* as

---

36. Volf, "Eschaton, Creation," 132–33.
37. Volf, "Eschaton, Creation," 142.
38. Heiges, *Christian's Calling*, 49.
39. Volf, *Work in the Spirit*, 119.
40. Volf, *Work in the Spirit*, 111–12.

Christians."[41] Luther and Calvin both emphasize that all Christians have a particular calling and are bound by it. But what about the unemployed? Are they excluded from the kingdom? Volf's pneumatological understanding of work does not deprive the unemployed of spiritual gifts. It means that the unemployed are without work but free to use their gifts in other ways. His charism theology directly challenges the Calvinistic work ethic.

Luther bifurcates his vocational theology by advocating a particular calling to either ministry or secular work. Volf uses the term *inter*personal distribution of vocations. The pneumatological understanding of work operates *inter*personally; Christians can have multiple charisms that contribute to the church and the transformation of the world.[42] Something Volf and the Reformational theologians agree upon is that while God is the giver of gifts, the individual is accountable for developing their gifts, and leaders should mentor them through this process.[43] All have a stake in the new creation. This process parallels what was advocated at the start of the age of Enlightenment.

Volf's pneumatological theology is not always accepted with open arms. Dr. Lee Hardy, professor of philosophy at Calvin College and adjunct professor of philosophic theology at Calvin Theological Seminary, states that Volf's "idea of gifts" was present in the Calvinist doctrine of vocation.[44] This is a fair acknowledgment, but Volf's theology focuses on gifts rather than particular stations (Calvinist vocational theology) and shifts from creation to the eschaton, the last thing. Another more vocal Volf critic, Dr. Douglas J. Schuurman, requires a deeper exploration.

---

41. Volf, *Work in the Spirit*, 110; emphasis original.
42. Volf, *Work in the Spirit*, 156.
43. Volf, *Work in the Spirit*, 173.
44. Hardy, *Fabric of This World*, 82.

POSTMODERN (1900 TO PRESENT)

DOUG SCHUURMAN (1955-2020)

Dr. Douglas J. Schuurman, former professor of religion at St. Olaf College in Northfield, Minnesota, devoted much of his scholarly career to reviving the Protestant concept of vocation. Many of his publications centered on vocation, and he started a vocation program for students at St. Olaf. He advocates returning to the Reformational concept of vocation as defined by Luther and Calvin, which "*includes all aspects of cultural and social life*,"[45] not the narrow modern definition relating to career. "We must return to the expansive, religiously rich understanding of vocation in the Bible and the Reformation."[46]

Schuurman outlines three vocational themes. First, all aspects of life are holy. He rejects the medieval concept of vocation, which was restricted to monastic or ecclesial activities. It was Luther who first shattered this ecclesiastical vocational concept and advocated the holiness of all offices that exhibit love of neighbor. Second, duties are to be governed by God's will. Again, he shares Luther's theology that through a social office, one participates with God. Luther describes this as God's mask. And third, officials are God's representatives, ordained to exercise God's will through their office.[47]

Schuurman, like most Protestant theologians, supports the general form of God's calling to faith in Jesus Christ. He also supports the specific or particular calling where "by the power of the Holy Spirit, the call becomes a living reality in the life of each individual."[48] He breaks with Volf's theology founded on gifts and eschatology. He also breaks with Barth's theology of leading a worthy life after accepting the general call. Schuurman's vocational theology cascades God's call to faith down into "concrete social locations one presently occupies."[49]

---

45. Schuurman, *Vocation*, 51; emphasis original.
46. Schuurman, *Vocation*, 4.
47. Schuurman, *Vocation*, 5-8.
48. Schuurman, *Vocation*, 25-26.
49. Schuurman, *Vocation*, 29.

In a 1995 *Calvin Theological Journal* article, he responded to Volf's publication *Work in the Spirit*. While he praises Volf's connection between postmodern work and the eschatological future, he advocates a more *balanced* theology rather than a theology focused on pneumatology and eschatology. "My rejoinder to Volf is that all the candidates for the center [of the New Testament] are also ecclesiological, or Christological, or soteriological, or covenantal, in nature."[50] Schuurman argues that his protological framework is not static, as claimed by Volf, but a transformative process and futuristic. Rather than elevating one theological theme over other themes, defined as "bracketing,"[51] Schuurman retains the traditional Protestant vocational theology founded upon protology.

Schuurman agrees with Volf's extension of Pauline ecclesiology to all spheres of social life. However, when examining 1 Cor 7:17–24, Schuurman remains neutral; he does not directly address Luther's exegetical error that a Christian should remain in their station.[52] Rather, in a section on relations among social spheres, he notes that the Puritan stance to strictly adhere to one's calling (1 Cor 7:20) may sound conservative, but "it can become reformist, or even revolutionary, when it is aimed at a totalitarian state."[53] In another section on expanded vocational choices, he acknowledges that modern vocational challenges were "only remotely of concern to Luther and Calvin." He then backtracks and states that these modern concerns apply only to middle- and upper-class individuals. Vocational freedom is restricted to a select few globally. He terms this *ascriptivism*.[54] Schuurman subscribes to Luther's cross of vocation theology, in which duty to God overrules self-fulfillment. Gifts are to be used for the common good rather than strictly for individual enjoyment.[55] Gifts

50. Schuurman, *Response to Volf*, 146.
51. Schuurman, *Response to Volf*, 152.
52. Schuurman, *Vocation*, 32–34.
53. Schuurman, *Vocation*, 103.
54. Schuurman, *Vocation*, 119.
55. Schuurman, *Vocation*, 123–24.

permeate an individual's particular calling and assist in tasks within society and the church.[56]

How does an individual determine their particular calling? Schuurman states that God does not have a predetermined blueprint for each person, but "God's providence provides comfort by leading us to the humble self-understanding that as finite, limited beings God calls us only to do our part, at this time and in this place."[57] He offers practical guidelines based on market supply and demand. If there are gluts of doctors and lawyers, then Christians should investigate shortages in other fields[58] and consult others for God's direction.[59] This advice sounds reasonable when placed within Volf's pneumatological theology but does not align with Luther's definition of particular calling. Schuurman and Volf both agree that God gives individuals gifts to be used in service to the community. What happens to Schuurman's vocational theology when economic markets change and a person is left unemployed and needs to change fields? He acknowledges the rapidly changing societal landscape yet is not being consistent with his premise related to particular calling. Our next theologian addresses these theological gaps.

GARY BADCOCK (BORN 1961)

Dr. Gary D. Badcock, professor emeritus of theology at Huron University College (London, Ontario), is a Canadian theologian who graduated with a doctor of philosophy from the University of Edinburgh. He previously taught in the UK and published *The Way of Life: A Theology of Christian Vocation* (1998) after Volf's *Work in the Spirit* (1990) and before Schuurman's *Vocation* (2004). Badcock agrees with both Volf and Schuurman on God's general calling to faith in Jesus Christ and that there is no

---

56. Schuurman, *Vocation*, 39.
57. Schuurman, *Vocation*, 46.
58. Schuurman, *Vocation*, 140–42.
59. Schuurman, *Vocation*, 150.

biblical connection to secular work or employment. As for 1 Cor 7:17–24, "the calling in verse 20 is not the calling '*with* which, *to* which, or *by* which a man is called, but refers to the state in which he is *when* he is called by God to become a Christian.'"[60] He disagrees with Luther's exegesis. He states "that use of the word *calling* in the Bible does not appear to support the naïve vision of the Christian life with which this book, and indeed much of my own early religious training, began." He concludes that the Bible is silent on career choices, and at best, vocation is only a derivative.[61] God does not give individuals a blueprint for their lives but the freedom to choose.[62]

Badcock asks an important question: "What will I do with my life?"[63] This question is the focus of his book as he blazes a different theological trail than Volf and Schuurman. Surprisingly, he directly answers this question: "It does not matter greatly. One does not disobey God by choosing any one worthwhile secular occupation over another, or by retiring at sixty rather than at sixty-five."[64] Badcock's theology destresses the individual searching for God's particular calling. He acknowledges that in the Bible, some individuals are called for special tasks, although this is the exception and not the rule.[65] However, he doesn't let the Christian totally off the hook. Badcock's vocational concept is to live a full human life; not to do so is to deny one's humanity.[66] Vocation is to do the will of God, which is revealed in Scripture.[67] God gives Christians the freedom to use their individual gifts, circumstances, and opportunities to devise a path through life.[68]

---

60. Badcock, *Way of Life*, 7; emphasis original.
61. Badcock, *Way of Life*, 9.
62. Badcock, *Way of Life*, 53.
63. Badcock, *Way of Life*, 10.
64. Badcock, *Way of Life*, 126.
65. Badcock, *Way of Life*, 82–83.
66. Badcock, *Way of Life*, 13.
67. Badcock, *Way of Life*, 15.
68. Badcock, *Way of Life*, 127.

After answering his first question, Badcock proposes a more important question: "What sort of person ought I to be?"[69] He answers it with Micah's words:[70] "He has told you, O mortal, what is good; and what does the Lord require of you but to do justice, and to love kindness, and to walk humbly with your God?" (Mic 6:8) Christians are to integrate their life journey into the overall mission of Christ:[71] "The call is to the love of God, and because God is love, to the love of one's neighbor."[72] This way of life "involves self-denial and often leads through suffering,"[73] which corresponds to Luther's cross of vocation. Badcock greatly simplifies vocational theology by giving Christians the freedom to choose social roles, careers, and nonpaid activities under the umbrella of love and service. It is sanctification after justification. It is living as Jesus Christ lived. "It has to do with what one lives 'for' rather than with what one does."[74]

We have come full circle. Scripture speaks of vocation as the call of God to faith in Jesus Christ. In rare cases, God calls a specific person to perform tasks, but most Christians do not have an undeniable encounter with God; the call of God does not cascade down to offices, careers, employment, or social roles. Our God-given gifts are to be used to show love of neighbor for the common good. However, the call of God is a way of life that often involves self-denial and suffering. Over time, medieval Christianity applied God's call to ecclesiastic roles, which were deemed more valuable to God than nonecclesiastical roles. Luther's Reformational theology labeled all social roles that showed love to neighbors as pleasing to God. Unfortunately, Luther misinterpreted 1 Cor 7:17–24 and espoused remaining in your current *Stand*. Calvin followed Luther's theology but emphasized diligent and frugal work, which was exaggerated by the Puritan work ethic. The Puritans' productivity

69. Badcock, *Way of Life*, 128.
70. Badcock, *Way of Life*, 82.
71. Badcock, *Way of Life*, 136.
72. Badcock, *Way of Life*, 123.
73. Badcock, *Way of Life*, 141.
74. Badcock, *Way of Life*, 142.

generated wealth, which gradually transformed the broad biblical definition of vocation into its narrow, secular definition. By the age of Enlightenment, vocation had lost its spiritual connection and was reduced to those doing church work and secular jobs. Postmodern theologians have revived the Protestant whole-life vocational concept and taken it back to its original biblical roots. They emphasize the use of an individual's God-given gifts, as articulated by the apostle Paul: showing love within community as Christ lived and taught.

The historical journey of vocation ends with my definition of vocation. It is:

- The comprehensive life of a Christian after positively responding to God's call to faith in Jesus Christ
- The wholeness of life, relationships, and responsibilities[75]
- Integral to God's mission,[76] the basis for human identity, and the understanding of humanness itself[77]
- Everything that brings humans into relationships with other humans[78]
- Faithful obedience to God[79] and being set apart for God's purpose[80] to love and serve one's neighbor[81]
- Human life in the Holy Spirit,[82] with each believer bearing the fruit of the Spirit[83]

It is now time to expand upon Badcock's second question: "What will I do with my life?" I would like to rephrase his question: "How will I use my gifts (*charismata*)?" Part 2 will explore this question in three sections: self-actualization, community, and choices. I will propose a hexagonal *charismata* portfolio model

---

75. Garber, *Visions of Vocation*, 11.
76. Garber, *Visions of Vocation*, 18.
77. Guinness, *Call*, 20.
78. Hardy, *Fabric of This World*, 111–2.
79. Marshall, *Kind of Life*, 24.
80. Denver Institute, *Study on Calling*.
81. Veith, *God at Work*, 39–40.
82. Badcock, *Way of Life*, 123.
83. Schuurman, *Vocation*, 26.

Postmodern (1900 to Present)

that balances a person's daily life and discusses habits and practices that reinforce held values.

PART II

Charismata and Vocation

Charismata

SELF-ACTUALIZATION

In part 2 of my book *Trading with God*, I created a threefold, distinct, and interrelating theological model of work (fig. 1).

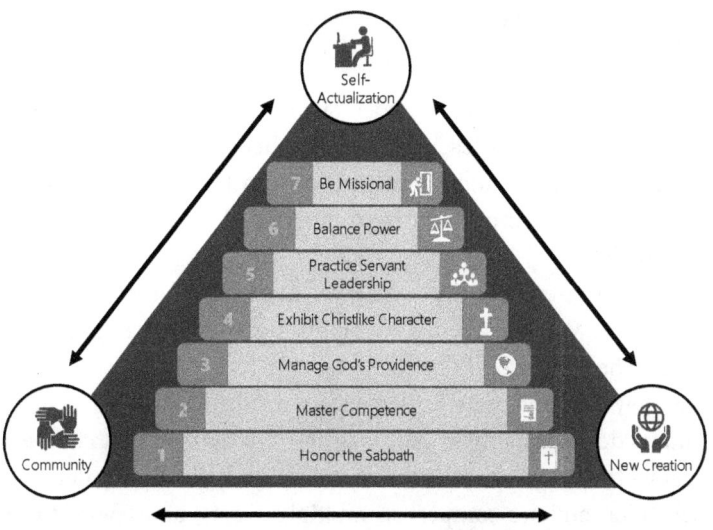

Figure 1—Theological Model of Work

One of the three aspects is self-actualization, based upon Maslow's hierarchy of human needs.[1] Self-actualization is the

---

1. See Maslow, "Theory of Human Motivation."

highest human need, where personal development is fully actualized using God-given gifts (*charismata*). Gifts are also deployed in the other four lower needs (physiological, safety, love/belonging, and esteem), but fully blossom in self-actualization.

Gifts

I have previously discussed gifts in part 1. In this section, I will concentrate on the practical aspects of gifts. Bill Hendricks, president of the Giftedness Center and developer of the term "giftedness," defines this term as:

> *The unique way in which you function. It's a set of inborn core strengths and natural motivation you instinctively and consistently use to do things that you find satisfying and productive. Giftedness is not just what you can do but what you are born to do, enjoy doing, and do well.*[2]

Dr. Parker Palmer, founder of the Center for Courage and Renewal, writes that "each of us arrives here with a nature, which means both limits and potentials. We can learn as much about our nature by running into our limits as by experiencing our potentials."[3]

It is self-evident that God gives humans different gifts. I attended the World Athletic Championship (WAC) in Eugene, Oregon, where the world's best athletes compete. As fast as sprinters are, they do not qualify for longer distance running events. Shot-putters do not qualify in pole vaulting. Hurdlers do not compete against the world's best javelin throwers. Only the heptathlon and decathlon athletes compete in multiple events, and few of these multi-event athletes can compete effectively at the WAC level in a single event. God created humans with a diversity of gifts.

Most humans use their gifts through specialization, a process that may cause great anxiety, as witnessed in young adults who struggle with selecting the right field of study or work and where to

---

2. Hendricks, *Person Called You*, 28; emphasis original.
3. Palmer, *Let Your Life Speak*, 41–42.

live or whom to marry. Some Christians believe that God predestined life decisions, so they stress over possibly making the wrong choice, thus shifting the responsibility of using their gifts to God.[4] This quest for finding the perfect match for your gifts, as though there is only one right choice, is self-defeating and inherently frustrating. The world is full of opportunities in which God-given gifts can be used.[5] God gives humans both gifts and free will.[6] Unless you have an undeniable encounter with God commanding a task (something rare in Scripture), relax—your choice does not matter, provided your gifts are used in love and service to your neighbors.[7] Barth states it best: "It is not required that he contribute much that is beautiful or out of the ordinary; it is required that he contribute what is his own, and that he do it totally, without dissimulation or embezzlement."[8] In freedom, decide how best to use your gifts.

Obtaining self-actualization is not an easy process. For a few extremely talented individuals, mastering a skill may be a quick and relatively easy process. For most mortals, gift proficiency requires hard, diligent work. For example, my nephew desired to be a professional trumpet performer. He was a good musician in high school and decided to pursue music as a career. He enrolled in a small college and was mentored by a national-level trumpet instructor. After four years of hard work, he enrolled in graduate schools and obtained a PhD in trumpet performance. Each year, he gained higher levels of musical competency. Upon graduation, gaining employment in this very competitive field was still challenging. He did make it into the Army's brass quintet, where he now performs in Washington, DC. "Mastering a vocation is more like digging a well. You do the same ... thing day after day, and gradually, gradually, you get deeper and better."[9]

---

4. Bernbaum and Steer, *Why Work*, 83.
5. Hardy, *Fabric of This World*, 91; Hendricks, *Person Called You*, 42.
6. Bernbaum and Steer, *Why Work*, 69.
7. Hardy, *Fabric of This World*, 80.
8. Barth, *Doctrine of Creation*, 627.
9. Brooks, *Second Mountain*, 127.

Charismata

The difficult work performed in developing gifts is not about gaining salvation, as previously discussed in the Protestant ethic section. There is a difference between rest and sloth. Laziness is neglecting your gifts, a form of disobedience to God.[10] Workaholics are just as unbalanced as slothful individuals. There is a path between the two extremes that leads towards a balanced self-actualization of God-given gifts. The Sabbath is a gift from God that balances work and rest. What is important is making the best use of gifts. Humans are finite beings and must understand that their time on earth is limited, something not to be wasted.[11]

Christ taught about using our gifts in the parable of the talents (Matt 25:14–30). The *master* is an analogy for God, *his slaves* are an analogy for humans, and *talents* (large sums of money worth more than fifteen years of a laborer's wages) are an analogy for *charismata*. Jesus expects his followers to use their God-given gifts while they wait for Jesus's return. The parable teaches us that it is not important to be the greatest producer, but rather to make the most of our gifts, great or small. The master was pleased with both slaves exhibiting different levels of productivity.[12] The slave who was idle and did not use his gifts received a severe punishment. The master was in charge and assigned the tasks, and the slaves were expected to use their gifts.[13] Jesus follows this parable with the judgment of the nations (Matt 25:31–46). Gifts are to be used in service to our neighbors. There will be a terrible cost when disobeyed: "And these will go away into eternal punishment but the righteous into eternal life" (Matt 25:46). Christians are commanded to serve during their short, uncertain earthly life.[14] We are not to delay using our gifts.

Supply and demand of gifts must be acknowledged and considered when making life choices. My nephew's trumpet performance choice was based on his musical gifts and desires. However,

---

10. Hendricks, *Person Called You*, 198.
11. Barth, *Doctrine of Creation*, 588.
12. Witherington, *Work*, 72.
13. Witherington, *Work*, 75.
14. Placher, *Callings*, 323.

he was fully aware that there were limited professional positions available; the competition is intense, and few obtain full-time employment as trumpet performers. Having a gift with the potential inability to use it in service needs to be considered during the selection process. One of the most-quoted definitions of vocation is by writer Frederick Buechner: "Neither the hair shirt nor the soft berth will do. The place God calls you to is the place where your deep gladness and the world's deep hunger meet."[15] I initially desired to go into medicine until I realized that very few applicants were accepted into medical schools. I decided to go into engineering, which also used my science-related gifts and provided a better chance of admittance. Both were acceptable choices.

Passion

Passion is a requirement for obtaining mastery of your gifts. It is very difficult to put in the requisite hard work for self-actualization without internal enjoyment, desire, and drive.[16] I never developed a driving passion for engineering. It equipped me with a good foundation for understanding technology, problem-solving, and project economics. I had more passion for business studies and energy trading, where most of my career was spent. I did not have a passion for the humanities until I worked and traveled internationally. My enjoyment of history, cultures, and literature blossomed later in life. I learned that passions evolve over time.[17] They wane and bloom with time and cannot be forced; passion comes from within. What are your passions that give you joy and continue to motivate you?[18] Only you can answer this question. "Faithfulness in vocation means positively that in my vocation as

---

15. Buechner, *Wishful Thinking*, 95.
16. Martin, *Between Heaven and Mirth*, 16.
17. Novak, *Business as a Calling*, 35.
18. Brooks, *Second Mountain*, 111.

it is I seek, either well or badly, to do satisfactory work to the best of my ability, skill, and conscience."[19]

During my third semester of engineering school, I took electromagnetic physics. This was the required weed-out course dreaded by all undergraduates. A Japanese professor taught it and told his students that their first exam grade would be their highest score. He advised his students to drop his class if they did poorly on the first exam. I scored a low B and struggled. I sought the advice of a talented upperclassman who gave me his class notes and old exams. I scored a low A on the next exam, and on the third exam, I scored a solid A. My professor wrote on my third exam: *Please come see me!* No professor had ever asked me to come to their office, and I dreaded the encounter. When I arrived, he said: "With each exam, you have scored higher. This is very unusual. I am impressed with your work. I would like you to consider becoming a physics major." I was in shock. The last thing I saw myself being was a physics major. I politely declined and gracefully exited his office. I had no passion for physics, and it was only through hard work (and perhaps some fear) that I succeeded in physics.

Guidance

What are my gifts, and how should I employ them?[20] Palmer, a Quaker, is an advocate of inner reflection. "Vocation does not come from a voice 'out there' calling me to become something I am not. It comes from a voice 'in here' calling me to be the person I was born to be, to fulfill the original selfhood given me at birth by God."[21] To understand your God-given gifts, personal reflection is important. But Palmer also advocates seeking community counsel as a counterpoint to strictly private reflection.[22] Seek counsel from trusted family and friends who have mature experiences, balanced

19. Barth, *Doctrine of Creation*, 642.
20. Hardy, *Fabric of This World*, 122.
21. Palmer, *Let Your Life Speak*, 10.
22. Palmer, *Let Your Life Speak*, 92.

judgment, and faithful character.[23] Seeking external guidance from others on gifts was recommended by Puritan leaders, such as Perkins and Baxter. "Choose no calling (especially if it be of public consequence) without the advice of some judicious, faithful persons of that calling."[24]

A small group of trusted individuals can operate as a discovery place for ideas and feedback.[25] Palmer advocates a "clearness committee," a process where group members can only ask questions and refrain from giving advice. It allows the seeker to discover truths themselves after being prodded with insightful questions.[26]

One controversial aspect of Palmer's inner or personal work is that it relies too heavily on human reasoning, a dangerous path given the state of fallen humanity.[27] If a person desires a life of crime, sexual immorality, or environmental harm, then withdrawing inwardly is self-destructive. God reveals what true life is through Scripture. In freedom, Christians should choose wisely, within the boundaries commanded by God. Scripture tells of individual encounters where God commands specific tasks, some daunting or life threatening. For example, Moses was told by God to stand up to Pharaoh and free the Hebrews from Egyptian slavery (Exod 3:1—4:17). Moses did not desire this task and told God that he did not have the required gifts necessary for success. God's summons came externally, not internally. God gave Moses and other chosen biblical figures the required gifts. Seeking direction on personal gifts, utilizing self-reflection and input from others, is wise counsel.[28] "The truth of our lives, as the proverbial saying goes, may lie 'somewhere in between,'"[29] as we balance external and internal conversations.

---

23. Hardy, *Fabric of This World*, 89; Schuurman, *Vocation*, 150.
24. Placher, *Callings*, 285.
25. Sherman, *Kingdom Calling*, 118–20.
26. Palmer, *Let Your Life Speak*, 44–46.
27. Schuurman, *Vocation*, 46.
28. Barth, *Doctrine of Creation*, 636.
29. Schwehn and Bass, *Leading Lives That Matter*, 457.

Examining my life after more than six decades, I should have sought more external counsel and spent more time internally wrestling. I did not ask hard questions nor use the abundance of human resources available to me. The journey would have been relatively easy given that both of my parents were college educated and networked with others in diverse fields. I had access to books, educators, and ministers who would gladly have assisted me with guidance related to my gifts. During my formative years, I did not readily seek direction. I floated along a single path.

During my engineering studies, I was fortunate to become friends with a church member who also happened to be an engineering professor at my school. We chatted about life in general, and I respected him. During my senior year, I asked him if he would recommend me as his student in the mineral and energy economics graduate degree program. He looked at me for a moment, smiled, and said: "I am looking for grasshoppers. You are a valuable ant, but not a grasshopper." His words were honest and spoken in love. Grasshoppers jump high and go far with each leap. Ants slowly plod away but can build great structures and eventually get to the same places as grasshoppers. My professor wanted grasshopper students. After six decades, I am still an ant.

COMMUNITY

The second aspect of the threefold, distinct, and interrelating theological model on faith and work is community. During my research, this aspect was by far the most discussed within vocational writings. The word community is derived from the Latin *communitas*, defined as "same," which was earlier derived from the Latin *communis*, which means "common, public, shared by all or many." Although gifts are typically viewed individualistically, they are deployed within community to serve others, both near and far. Jesus Christ had human and divine gifts, yet the focus of his mission was community. Vocation is relational; it is showing love and serving one's neighbors. Community balances self-actualization. There is always a tension between self and community, between individuals and groups.³⁰ Individualism is not only suboptimal, but ineffective and perhaps even destructive.

Citizenship

I wrote extensively about community in my first book, *Trading with God*. I will add three additional features to this important aspect. The first is *citizenship*. The United States and other Western countries have increasingly swung towards individualism. This book is not about describing the underlying causes for this shift, but the trend is troubling. Our Reformational heritage encourages citizenship, which is Christian participation in public groups and private nonprofits that serve the community. Our gifts should contribute to the public good,³¹ but using these gifts also contributes to a good life. While there can be additional stresses and tensions with citizenship, there is also joy in service.³² Christians are commanded to show love, gentleness, and kindness, even when the opposite is confronted.³³ Convictions and character are built within community, not in isolation.³⁴ Life is far better spent working on solutions rather than accepting problems.

Dr. Viktor Frankl (1905–97), an Austrian holocaust survivor and psychiatrist, wrote *Man's Search for Meaning*, the story of his concentration camp experiences. He was quoted as saying, to achieve personal meaning, one must transcend subjective pleasures by doing something that "points and is directed, to something, or someone, other than oneself ... by giving himself to a cause to serve or another person to love."³⁵

Christians can find personal meaning by participating in civic service; it transcends individualism, directs love towards

---

30. Brooks, *Second Mountain*, xvii.
31. Bellah et al., *Habits of the Heart*, 142.
32. Bellah et al., *Habits of the Heart*, 196.
33. Brooks, *Second Mountain*, 310.
34. Garber, *Fabric of Faithfulness*, 159–60.
35. Winslade, "Afterword," 159.

humanity, and acts as a societal counterbalance to those who seek only personal gains.

Responsibility

The second community feature is *responsibility*. Dr. Dietrich Bonhoeffer (1906–45), Lutheran pastor and theologian, deeply understood responsibility within community. He wrote his bestselling book, *The Cost of Discipleship*, after the Nazi Gestapo closed his underground Confessing Church seminary. In 1939, Bonhoeffer traveled to the United States at the invitation of Union Theological Seminary. He was urged to stay in the safety of New York City but declared that he could not live outside of Germany while German Christians faced terrible trials inside his militarized country. When he returned to Germany, he decided to work undercover as a courier for the German resistance movement. In 1943, Bonhoeffer was arrested and placed in Tegel Prison, Berlin, while awaiting trial. When it was discovered that Bonhoeffer was connected to the Abwehr conspiracy to kill Hitler, he was executed at the Flossenbürg concentration camp a month prior to Germany's defeat by Allied military forces. He lived a life of community responsibility and wrote: "Vocation is the place at which one responds to the call of Christ and thus lives responsibly. The task given to me by my vocation is thus limited; but my responsibility to the call of Jesus Christ knows no bounds."[36] For Bonhoeffer, freely answering Christ's call is to be responsible within community. Barth, who had a close relationship with Bonhoeffer, states that vocation is the point of origin, the fulfillment of God's command to love God and your neighbor as yourself.[37]

We are born at a certain point in history. We do not know what will happen during our short earthly existence. Although we have little control of our historical setting, we still occupy a place

---

36. Schwehn and Bass, *Leading Lives That Matter*, 109.
37. Barth, *Doctrine of Creation*, 598.

of responsibility in relation to others.[38] A fundamental question must be asked when making life choices. Will I be able to use my gifts responsibly in the service of others?[39] The majority of Christians do not face the extraordinary life-or-death decisions that Bonhoeffer faced during wartime Germany. However, responsibility still resides within everyday life. God's call is to a life of faith; responsibility is the lifetime sphere of God's call.[40]

Vaclav Havel (1936–2011), Czech statesman and playwright, was imprisoned multiple times by Communist authorities for his writings and political beliefs. His leadership led to the Velvet Revolution, which toppled the Czech Communist government. He was elected president of Czechoslovakia in 1989 by the unanimous vote of the Federal Assembly. Havel writes: The "secret of man is the secret of his responsibility."[41] Making choices about the use of gifts is important, perhaps leading to negative personal consequences. Some face the prospect of death and die, like Bonhoeffer. Others face the prospect of death and live to see a brighter future, like Havel. Both understood that vocation is responsibility that involves making the right response to God's call when using individual gifts within community.

Common Good

Building upon the first two community themes of *citizenship* and *responsibility*, the third is *common good*. Responding positively to God's call, our vocation leads to using our gifts as a contribution to the common good of all.[42] Although individuals possess different gifts, all are called to use their gifts for the common good.[43] The apostle Paul illustrates the use of spiritual gifts in 1 Cor 12–14,

---

38. Barth, *Doctrine of Creation*, 623.
39. Hardy, *Fabric of This World*, 124.
40. Guinness, *Call*, 87.
41. Garber, *Visions of Vocation*, 95.
42. Bellah et al., *Habits of the Heart*, 66.
43. Hardy, *Fabric of This World*, 60.

which by analogy can be expanded to all God-given gifts. As previously detailed, Calvin advocates the Reformational belief that callings are to be employed for the common good. Puritans gave firm directions to their members: "The principal thing to be intended in the choice of a trade or calling for yourselves or children, is the service of God, and the public good, and therefore (other things being equal) that calling which most conduceth to the public good is to be preferred."[44] In more recent history, Volf's pneumatological vocational theology revolves around God's call, individual gifts, and the common good.[45] From Scripture through to the present, a consistent theme is for God's people to work for the common good. Self-actualization must be bolted onto community; gifts must be bolted onto the common good.

Dr. Timothy Keller (1950–2023), founding pastor of Redeemer Presbyterian Church in New York City, gave a sermon series on Proverbs titled "True Wisdom for Living." His January 16, 2005, sermon, "Creation Care and Justice," encapsulates building community around the common good. Keller founded Redeemer Presbyterian Church in urban Manhattan, known more for ruthless corporate life than church attendance. Yet Redeemer has flourished while advocating Calvinist theology despite being surrounded by urban professionals heavily influenced by secular values.

He also preached on Prov 11:10: "When it goes well with the righteous, the city rejoices, and when the wicked perish, there is jubilation." The Hebrew word for "righteous" is *tsaddiqim* (singular: *tsaddiq*). The *tsaddiqim* are those who carry out God's will and are assumed to be Jewish spiritual leaders. When a righteous person rises to the top of their field, the city rejoices and does not resent their success. A victory for the *tsaddiqim* is a victory for all. *Tsaddiqim* prosperity entails weaving back shalom into the community for the common good of all. Where there are inequitable distributions of opportunities and resources in the world, the *tsaddiqim* work for the common good and the community rejoices. Where

---

44. Placher, *Callings*, 283.
45. Volf, *Work in the Spirit*, 199.

there are injustices, the *tsaddiqim* bring justice and the community rejoices. "The righteous in the book of Proverbs are by definition those who are willing to disadvantage themselves for the community while the wicked are those who put their own economic, social, and personal needs ahead of the needs of the community."[46]

This text is counterintuitive. Corporate and political organizations are designed to advocate for their particular causes, many at the expense of other groups of people. Success is normally tied to individuals prospering, not the entire community. But when the righteous prosper, by placing their own needs secondary to communal needs, the community celebrates. *Tsaddiqim* are those who carry out God's will, not human selfish desires. Keller preached to current and future Manhattan leaders and instructed them in God's way, not their surrounding cultural norms. He was juxtaposing God's common good against individualism.

CHOICES

The third aspect of the threefold, distinct, and interrelating theological model on faith and work is the new creation. The world caught a glance of it in Jesus Christ, but the new creation is not yet here on earth. Christians look forward towards the fulfillment of the new creation. In part 1, Badcock changed the vocation question from "What ought I to do?" to "What kind of person ought I to be?" He believed that a Christian's decisive consideration should be integration with the mission of Jesus Christ.[47] This may involve suffering and self-denial. The focus on *doing* is secondary to what one lives *for*.[48] This involves making choices. There will be many choices along the journey of developing and deploying gifts. Badcock states that when making choices, the deciding factors should be: (1) What sort of person should I be? (2) How should I choose

---

46. Sherman, *Kingdom Calling*, 16–17.
47. Badcock, *Way of Life*, 136.
48. Badcock, *Way of Life*, 142.

to live? and (3) What sense of fulfillment do I desire?[49] Gifts are given from the abundant goodness of God. Their deployment can be either towards building the new creation or evil destruction.[50] Choose wisely and prayerfully.

Moral Life

I will discuss five important choices that a person usually confronts along their journey. The first is the moral life. During my engineering undergraduate and my business graduate studies, there were no required ethics courses, and I did not take an ethics class as an elective. While in seminary, I was required to take an ethics course and I looked forward to the class. I wanted to have an ethical checklist that would ensure that I lived a moral, Christian life. To my disappointment, we read from various historical writers who primarily discussed ethics that related to classical philosophy, economics, race, environmental, and other issues. I came away disillusioned. One fellow seminary student said just before graduation: "We rarely discussed during my three years what it means to be obedient to God." The moral life is being obedient to God daily. Morality is not an abstract philosophical checklist.[51] After having accepted God's call, it is living a life commanded by the Creator, Redeemer, and Sustainer.

I usually know that I am not leading a moral life when I start to feel uncomfortable about my actions. Even if my actions were perfectly legal and perhaps personally beneficial, when my conscience bothers me, I know I have crossed the line and am not living the life of my calling. I start to ask questions: "What would my mother think?," "What if a reporter printed this?," and "What would Jesus Christ say to me?" The answer usually comes back: *don't do it.*

---

49. Badcock, *Way of Life*, 130.
50. Hendricks, *Person Called You*, 55.
51. Novak, *Business as a Calling*, 49.

The Christian life has moral boundaries that are found in Scripture. In today's declining Western Christianity, there is an absence of objectifiable criteria as a moral guide. Unless there is a law forbidding an action, it can be done and perhaps encouraged. Just turn on the TV, watch Netflix, or listen to pop music; the criteria between right and wrong, good and evil, self and community, have blurred so much that there are few, if any, moral boundaries.[52] Many of our social ills are not political or economic, but seeded in immorality.[53] Where there is no moral compass, the sort of person I ought to be becomes utterly meaningless. There is no meaning to life. Humans are then just another evolutionary earthly creature where the most powerful survive and rule over the weak.

Truth is found in God's revealed word, for with God, there are boundaries and meaning as followers of Christ. "God, and God alone, certifies and establishes an objective moral order, which is necessary for orienting ourselves ethically in ways that transcend matters of mere legality, opinion and culture. God's commands, based on God's unchangingly good character, determine morality."[54] Building our moral character requires practicing habits of virtues. Just as a person goes daily to a gym to build muscles and stamina for long-term physical health, Christian moral habits are strengthened through long-term discipleship. Just as a healthy person eats nutritious food and resists eating junk food, Christians strengthen their character and resist moral vices through worship, prayer, and avoiding compromising environments.[55] The ethic of Christian character is propelling one's calling into how one lives.[56] This is the moral life.

---

52. Bellah et al., *Habits of the Heart*, 76.
53. Bellah et al., *Habits of the Heart*, 295.
54. Groothuis, *Truth Decay*, 209–10.
55. Novak, *Business as a Calling*, 159.
56. Garber, *Fabric of Faithfulness*, 48.

Culture

The second choice, closely related to moral life, is culture. When I first lived as an expat in London, my employer sent me to a company course on cultures. It was taught by a man who had done statistical analyses on cultures and developed key cultural attributes. Different cultures were placed on a linear attribute scale that varied between extremes. For example, one attribute is time. The Chinese view the time horizon as long term while Americans see time as short term. China has dealt with Taiwan for many years with the ultimate, long-term goal of reunification with mainland China. They conduct business using the same approach. Americans want solutions now. Unless there is a quick victory, Americans get impatient and when issues do not get resolved quickly, they look for a graceful exit. Vietnam, Iraq, and Afghanistan are recent examples. There are other cultural attributes, such as decision-making (horizontal or pyramid) and orientation (community or individualism), which help individuals, governments, and corporations understand and navigate cultures. I learned to appreciate these cultural nuances during my personal and professional experiences.

Christianity, since its earliest beginning, struggled against culture. Acts 6:1–7 is the first recorded conflict. From the Roman culture to the recent United Methodist Church division on sexuality, culture is an enduring problem for Christians. The clash is primarily between reason and revelation. Does one follow rational human knowledge or the will of God?[57] Jesus Christ battled culture when he taught about the kingdom of God in contrast to the evil surrounding him. This clash led to his crucifixion.

Culture is what humans superimpose on the natural world. It includes everything that is created by humans: languages, customs, values, social organizations, technical innovations, etc. Culture always comprises social aspects and human achievements, both from the mind and hands. It centers around values; what is good is always what is good for humans.[58] Humans can never escape

---

57. Niebuhr, *Christ and Culture*, 10–11.
58. Niebuhr, *Christ and Culture*, 32–35.

culture, although many have tried, as I articulated in part 1 on monasticism. Humans are a product of their location, family, social status, historical setting, and education. They are influenced by their surroundings, including both good and bad environments. We all breathe the same air and move around the same earth, a fact that can greatly influence our very being. Culture is created by humans, but humans are not culture. Humans still make choices within culture.[59]

There are people who blame their life decisions on culture: neighbors, schools, family members, friends, governments, etc. These cultural realities do influence one's life journey, but they should not define their calling or gifts. Frankl, a Jew placed in a Nazi concentration camp, suffered like millions of Jews, from Nazi cruelty. Yet he was not consumed by his culture. "If there is a meaning in life at all, then there must be a meaning in suffering. ... Everywhere man is confronted with fate, with the chance of achieving something through his own suffering."[60] Bonhoeffer and Barth stood up to the Nazis and suffered consequences for their faith. Christians are not controlled by their historical situations. When occupying our time in history, a Christian "bears responsibility for what will be made of it."[61]

Niebuhr gave a series of January 1949 lectures at Austin Presbyterian Theological Seminary on culture. In 1951, his lectures were published in a book, *Christ and Culture*, still a classic after more than seventy years. Niebuhr developed five motifs or thematic elements to show a range of ways that Christians deal with culture. He scales his motifs between theological revelation and philosophic reason. On the revelation extreme are the radicals (Christ against culture), and opposite are the reason extreme, the culturists (Christ of culture). Within these two extremes, sliding from revelation towards reason, are synthesists (Christ above culture), dualists (Christ and culture in paradox), and conversionists (Christ the transformer of culture). Most Christians align in the

---

59. Barth, *Doctrine of Creation*, 620–21.
60. Frankl, *Man's Search for Meaning*, 67–68.
61. Barth, *Doctrine of Creation*, 623.

middle motifs and there is no thematic element that is the definitive Christian answer to culture; all have theological truths and errors.[62] How does one choose? For Niebuhr, it "is not whether we will choose in accordance with reason or by faith, but whether we will choose with reasoning faithlessness or reasoning faith."[63]

There are some people who stated that the postmodern church has been influenced more by culture than the church has influenced the surrounding culture.[64] If one examines the totality of Christian history, my perspective is that it is a tied game. Like tidal currents, cultural influences ebb and flow over time. Currently, the paths of culture are flowing away from Christianity's power over Western culture. Individualism and human reasoning are making cultural gains.

Andy Crouch, a partner for theology and culture at Praxis, believes that our culture is the accumulated product of the past. *"The only way to change culture is to create more of it."*[65] He is a conversionist, a transformer of culture within culture,[66] which begins with an individual's calling and gifts.[67] For example, instead of boycotting offensive movies, support movies and activities that exhibit the moral life. I enjoy listening to classical music, family TV shows, and Shakespearean plays that support my faith-based values. There are many alternatives in culture that one can support and grow.

John Wesley (1703–91), an Anglican minister and founder of Methodism, was a conversionist. He tried to transform the Church of England from within but was rejected and shunned. Instead of accepting the culture of English Christianity, he followed the Spirit in mission to the working-class population left behind by the Church of England elites. He preached to tens of thousands in open fields, ministered to those impacted by the social ills of the

62. Niebuhr, *Christ and Culture*, 231.
63. Niebuhr, *Christ and Culture*, 251.
64. Whelchel, *How Then*, 86; Witherington, *Work*, 123.
65. Crouch, *Culture Making*, 67; emphasis original.
66. Crouch, *Culture Making*, 179.
67. Crouch, *Culture Making*, 196–97.

industrial age, and traveled by horse throughout rural England. He also endured mobs who pelted him with objects and threatened his life. He said that the world was his parish. Today, the motto of the United Methodist Church is "Making Disciples of Jesus Christ for the Transformation of the World."[68]

Rather than trying to change your surrounding culture, be the leaven of Christ in your community. Become a culture maker rather than a culture absorber. This requires discipline and sometimes difficult choices. As I grew older and witnessed the transition into the age of social media, I realized how easy it is for youths to be captured by the prevailing winds of culture. There are few boundaries to shield them as they make sense of their world. Loving guidance within a faith community is so necessary, now more than ever. Exhibit the fruits of the Spirit (Gal 5:22–26) when deploying your gifts and watch the Spirit transform culture. This was the mission of Jesus and look what happened.

Money

Entwined in the first two choices is the third choice: money. When I was in seminary, I took a course on the theology of money. We studied Scripture and found verses that condemn and praise money. The Bible isn't clear on money and wealth. Christ condemned the love of money (Matt 6:24), but still used it as currency for purchases (Matt 22:17–21). Money is just an efficient means of exchange invented by humans. By itself, it is not evil or harmful. It is the improper use of money by humans that is evil (1 Tim 6:6–10). Truth, character, and joy come from God, not money.[69] No amount of money can ever satisfy,[70] something I witnessed while working in energy trading.

---

68. Alexander, *Book of Discipline*, 91.
69. Claar and Klay, *Economics in Christian Perspective*, 45.
70. Hendricks, *Person Called You*, 39.

There are those who have written that vocational choices should not involve money.[71] I disagree. Each person has a different financial comfort level.[72] I desired an income that allowed me to live in a safe neighborhood with good schools for my children. I desired an income that allowed me to save for my children's higher education, a retirement pension, and adequate medical insurance. When making occupational choices, I steered towards higher-paying jobs that aligned with my gifts and desired standard of living. I could have sought lower-paying employment, but I was uncomfortable with that income choice. My employment choices contributed to the common good. I am at peace with my vocational decisions. One must find the correct balance between income and *charismata*. My older brother was content to live frugally during high school and university, as he preferred to spend his time in academic pursuits. I sought summer jobs in energy that both paid well and provided me with valuable industry skills. Financial comfort level is different for everyone and there is a wide spectrum of options. When a person disregards money when making vocational choices, it may lead to unhappiness and bitterness.

Success

Tied to money is the pursuit of success, another passionate goal with a broad span of meanings. The world generally determines personal worth through achievements.[73] Many people track the lives of the mega-wealthy, especially the young billionaires who obtained their fortunes early, and seek to emulate their journeys to fame and fortune without a thought towards the common good. Nonprofits clamor for their philanthropy. Financial institutions pursue them for capital investments. Success for success's sake leads to disappointment and unhappiness.[74] If the goal or

---

71. Guinness, *Call*, 135; Hendricks, *Person Called You*, 105; Albion, *Making a Life*, 232.
72. T. Nelson, *Work Matters*, 157.
73. Marshall et al., *Labour of Love*, 68.
74. Frankl, *Man's Search for Meaning*, xiv–xv.

cause is worthy, then humbly journey towards it without seeking success. While achieving a worthy goal may bring external praise and publicity, these should remain on the perimeter and can be a distraction.[75] It is the common good benefits that bring internal satisfaction, not money or press clippings.

Those with extraordinary gifts view success as obtaining the highest levels in their respective fields. For example, Olympic athletics view an Olympic gold medal as success. When I watched the world's best athletes compete, I could not imagine achieving their feats, but I did not envy their athletic talent. For me, my goals were relative to my level of local competition. I learned from their superb skills, but satisfaction was measured by a standard related to my natural talents and aptitudes, not absolute world records. I would always be a failure if I compared myself to elite world standards and I always knew that my gifts were not at the highest levels. God gives gifts to humans but does not distribute them evenly. This does not mean that God loves those with extraordinary gifts more than those with average talents. Quite the contrary: God's love is not based on our merits. Rather, it is evenly distributed; all are created in the image of God. The unskilled laborer is equal in God's eye to the president of the United States. We are all successful and equally loved when we declare our faith in Jesus Christ. It is only humans who differentiate people into categories of success, often based on wealth or personal gifts. God has a different standard.

Location

The fourth choice is location, the place where your *charismata* is deployed. During my college senior year, I interviewed for engineering jobs. I would sign up for one-hour campus interviews and, if successful, would later be asked to spend a day interviewing at a company site. I was always asked, "Are there any locations where you do not want to work?" One interviewer blurted out, "So you

---

75. Hendricks, *Person Called You*, 27.

also want to work only in Colorado?" It seemed that many of my fellow seniors desired jobs only in Colorado. It is a beautiful state!

I had worked the summer after my freshman year in Bakersfield, California, and always told prospective employers that I did not wish to work in Bakersfield. After one campus interview, I was offered a site visit to Bakersfield. I called the recruiter and inquired why they were sending me to Bakersfield after I had stated I had no desire to work there. The recruiter said that I would do only a one-year training assignment there, then be transferred to another location. I did not accept their site visit. After having spent three summer months in Bakersfield, I had already done my training assignment and was eager to live elsewhere.

Like money, decisions related to residence may seem inconsequential. If one is passionate about their work, then where one lives may not be a high priority. Again, I disagree. Like money choices, location choices need to be balanced. I found Bakersfield to be an unsuitable environment for me after having worked there for only three months. I had other suitable options and was able to choose different locations. I have worked with people who are employed around New York City, and they would never contemplate living in Texas. I would not exchange locations with them, nor they with me. I loved my London expat assignments but had no desire to live there permanently. I balanced my London work assignments with the negatives of being far away from family and friends. Others told me they could never leave their existing location due to elderly parents, children's schooling, or cost of living. In the 1997 movie *Good Will Hunting*, the main character is a genius who values his neighborhood and friends over his career; remaining in a construction job within his current neighborhood took precedence over a professional career.[76] All these factors play a part in deciding on a location. It is rare for a person to have it all.

Technology has enabled more people to work remotely, which has given people more flexibility to choose their location. I have witnessed both of my children having more location options in their lives than I experienced, primarily due to technology

---

76. Schwehn and Bass, *Leading Lives That Matter*, 323.

advances. This has improved their quality of life, especially by living in lower-cost communities and commuting less. All these factors need to be considered when choosing how to use God's gifts. There is no perfect location but there should be one that is balanced with your other choices. Sometimes, locations are temporary and can be changed when deemed unsuitable. Most of us have our Bakersfields. Just don't stay too long if relocation is an option.

Leisure

The fifth and final important choice is rest and leisure activities: sports, hobbies, and fellowship. In our workaholic, capitalist-focused society, this fundamental aspect of life gets neglected by many people. The first step is honoring the Sabbath and keeping the day holy, commanded upon the faithful through Mosaic laws that Jesus followed. During my childhood, most stores were closed and people generally went to church and remained home on Sunday afternoons. Gradually, Sunday became like any other day of the week. I mourn these societal changes. A day of rest and reflection rejuvenates the body, both physically and mentally. I worked on Sundays afternoons in high school and college, something I now deeply regret. I was in a rush to earn money and should have arranged my employment within the first six days of the week. Over time, I came to appreciate the Sabbath and how good it is for humans. It is a gift from God for the well-being of humankind.

Leisure activities give balance to our lives and must be taken into consideration when making vocational choices. Music, artistic creation, sports, and hobbies can be performed around demanding careers, but only through planning and finding balance. Families with children who participate in leisure activities will also need to make choices. Location decisions may need adjusting to accommodate leisure. If one is an avid golfer, then living in southern climates may be a priority. If one loves winter sports, then living in northern or mountainous climates may be required. When my daughter showed gymnastic potential, we contemplated moving to a different part of Houston to be near an Olympic gymnastic coach. After much agonizing, the choice was made to remain in our community.

Some *work to live* and others *live to work*. Rest and leisure activities are important choices. Total focus on either end of the work-leisure spectrum is potentially harmful. Not prioritizing the Sabbath elevates the material world over the ultimate true God. Leisure activities build physical and mental strength that add balance to our vocation. I chose running and reading nonfiction as my leisure activities. Competitive running gave me physical endurance and destressed me prior to heading to work. After the kids were in bed, I relaxed with a book before going to sleep. There is not a perfect solution that applies to all people. Choices must be made, and balance sought.

Vocation

CHARISMATA PORTFOLIO

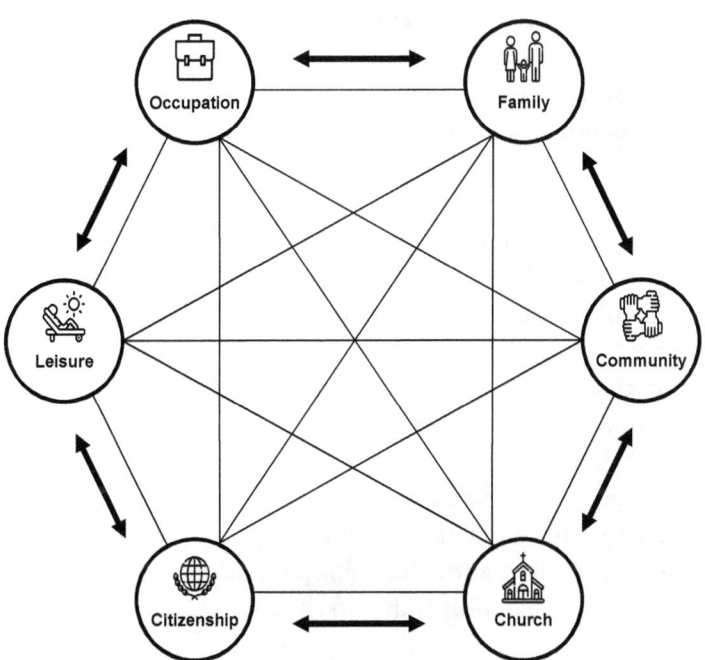

Figure 2—*Charismata* Portfolio Model

I took an investments course during my MBA studies and was fascinated by it. One of the topics was diversification: reducing risk by creating a balanced portfolio of different investments. If a person invests in only one equity (for example, General Motors), then the investment is subject to the market forces of only one stock, be it good or bad. If a person invests in twenty equities that are derived from various market segments (energy, technology, medical, transportation, etc.), then risk is reduced through diversification versus a single stock portfolio. Most investors don't want to lose all their capital by betting on a single investment. Although there may be great gains, there may also be great losses. Spreading capital over a broad range of investments is usually a more balanced, safer financial position for long-term investing.

Investment portfolio theory can be applied to *charismata*, the use of God-given gifts within vocation. Figure 2 illustrates a hexagonal *charismata* portfolio model that contains six important aspects of life: occupation, family, community, church, citizenship, and leisure. I have stressed in the choices section that balance is very important when making life decisions. Those who place all their time and resources into a single aspect are what E. M. Forster (1879-1970), an English writer, described as *flat people*, defined as having only one dimension in their life. He preferred *rounded (portfolio) people*.[1] For flat people, not only is there a higher probability of failure or burnout, but an individual's complete development will be limited to a single aspect. If a person spends all their time within a church environment, then that individual cannot easily relate to many of the people in the world who are not Christian or do not devote much of their time to a church. A single-portfolio person becomes not only *flat* but is at risk when change occurs during their lifetime. Many theologians and vocational writers have advocated being portfolio people.[2] *Charismata* are not associated solely with work, whether secular or spiritual.

---

1. Higginson, *Questions of Business Life*, 258.

2. Bellah et al., *Habits of the Heart*, 69, 220; Bennethum, *Listen*, 20, 66; Bernbaum and Steer, *Why Work*, 83; Garber, *Visions of Vocation*, 28, 198; Groothuis, *Truth Decay*, 277-79; Hardy, *Fabric of This World*, 113,118; Heiges, *Christian's Calling*, 49; Higginson, *Questions of Business Life*, 258-76; Kolden, "Luther on Vocation," 383-84; Mackenzie and Kirkland, *Where's God on Monday*, 93; Mackenzie et al., *Soul Purpose*, 16; Paul S. Minear, in J. Nelson, *Work and Vocation*, 50; Schuster, *Answering Your Call*, 27; Sherman, *Kingdom Calling*, 48; Schuurman, *Vocation*, xiii, 109; Whelchel, *How Then*, 76; Wuthnow,

VOCATION

The six aspects of my proposed *charismata* model are interdependent, not independent. Each aspect relates to the others.[3] For example, occupation affects community, family, leisure, church, and citizenship. Time spent working means time not taken with family, friends, sports, volunteering, or citizenship. Harmony is sought within the *charismata* portfolio. There are periods in life when aspects get out of balance. For example, a family member needs assistance due to an injury or sickness. One may need to devote considerable time tending to this family member, which takes time from other aspects. This is understandable for certain periods of life but is not healthy for the long term. A return to a more balanced use of *charismata* is required for wholeness, personal growth, and stability.[4] A good illustration is of a tightrope walker balancing his or her muscles and the environmental elements to complete a journey over perilous terrain (hopefully with a safety net!). A less dramatic illustration is a musical composition that achieves harmonies within various themes, patterns, and tones. All contribute to a distinctive life through balance.[5]

Interdependence has its benefits. A work colleague may also be a member of your church or a fellow member of your community softball team. It was a church member who suggested that I apply for work at his employer. His recommendations led me into a long and enjoyable career in energy trading.

Community is found within each aspect, thus providing contacts or friends from diverse segments of life. Seeking a broad and diversified community of people enables exposure to varying opinions, experiencing multiple cultures, associating with ranges of ages and social levels, and interacting with different religions. If a person has only church friends, then one is not participating in the great commission (Matt 28:18–20). If a person derives all friendships from work colleagues, then leaving an employer or

---

Crisis in the Churches, 72.

3. Schwehn and Bass, *Leading Lives That Matter*, 184–6.

4. Mackenzie and Kirkland, *Where's God on Monday*, 93; Witherington, *Work*, 158; Wuthnow, *Crisis in the Churches*, 136.

5. Schwehn and Bass, *Leading Lives That Matter*, 454.

experiencing a business failure can be devastating.[6] A *charismata* portfolio spreads life's risks and rewards over more segments. The diversifying effect allows a person to use their gifts within multiple segments of life experiences. Narrowing *charismata* to only one or two aspects increases specialization but decreases the ability to change and adapt over time. During my lifetime, I have witnessed how fast technology has changed all aspects of life. A *charismata* portfolio allows a person to develop nimbleness and optionality during the journey of life.

ESTABLISHING HABITS

During my high school years, I studied just enough to be accepted into an engineering school. I did the required homework and prepared for exams, but schoolwork was not my passion. I worked mowing lawns to gain spending money, and upon turning sixteen years old, I worked at a nearby grocery store. I went to church on Sunday, participated in youth fellowship, played trumpet in the school band, and joined after-school activities. Through all these various activities, I developed habits: be punctual, complete assigned homework and family chores, attend Sunday church, save money, be home for dinner, and practice music.

When I went to university, I needed to develop new habits. The time for coursework greatly increased and required more preparation; no longer was a quick review adequate. I devoted most of my time to homework assignments, labs, projects, and test preparation. After weekday supper, I spent evenings studying until bedtime. Weekends were spent working at campus jobs or studying. To graduate, I needed discipline and focus. I still attended church, but not as often. I had little leisure time, physical activity, or recreation time until the semester was over. I did learn to focus on my education, as I wanted to be employed as a professional engineer.

---

6. Albion, *Making a Life*, 39.

Vocation

Upon graduation from higher education, I switched to full-time work and learned new habits. I was expected to arrive and depart my employer's office at regular hours, dress appropriately, complete assigned tasks, make presentations to my supervisor, and attend meetings. After work, I had to do other activities: shop for groceries, prepare food, wash clothes, clean the house, service my car, go to medical appointments, etc. My flexibility to alter this schedule was drastically reduced because I commuted and worked more than forty hours a week. As I married and my first child was born, my priorities changed again and new habits were developed: childcare, landscape maintenance, church activities, and exercise. My days were filled with balancing many life aspects; habits became even more important.

In 1991, I chanced upon Stephen Covey's (1932–2012) book *The Seven Habits of Highly Effective People*. It changed my life and enabled me to link my values and goals. I learned to create a personal mission statement, list my values, and develop priorities. I set yearly goals for the various aspects of my life that cascaded down into monthly and daily goals. Priorities (*a, b, c*) were placed next to each goal, and I focused on completing the highest priorities (*a*) first, followed by the next highest priorities (*b*), and if there was any remaining time, I would complete *c* priorities. Practicing habits that reinforce your values and balance life aspects are required to live a life of purpose and meaning. Each person is unique, but we all need to establish habits.

Alexis de Tocqueville (1805–59), a French political scientist, published *Democracy in America* (two volumes, 1835 and 1840). He coined the phrase "habits of the heart" to describe the American character:

> He singled out family life, our religious traditions, and our participation in local politics as helping to create the kind of person who could sustain a connection to a wider political community and thus ultimately support the maintenance of free institutions. He also warned that some aspects of our character—what he was one of the first to call "individualism"—might eventually isolate

Americans one from another and thereby undermine the conditions of freedom.[7]

Tocqueville identified community as an American foundational principle within our new nation. Community is a thread that flows throughout all aspects. Self-actualization is always balanced by community.

Rituals are part of habits:[8] beliefs that instill behaviors.[9] I pray daily after getting out of bed and dressing. The quiet early morning allows me to focus and prepare for the day's activities. I then exercise for an hour, either running outside or strength training in a gym. I eat breakfast every morning. These early-morning habits have existed since early adulthood. Sunday mornings are spent at church, which reminds me of God's command to rest and keep the Sabbath day holy (Deut 5:12). Studying Scripture enables God's word to speak to you.[10] I stay grounded by practicing ritual habits that match my stage of life.[11]

Church worship has ritual habits that were generated over two thousand years of Christian history: singing, responsive readings, Scripture, community prayer, preaching, choral music, communion, and meditation. Some denominational worship services are highly ritualized, while others are less structured. Rituals link postmodern Christians with the saints of the church universal. While each person is a unique individual, we share with other Christians our common love of Jesus Christ. Rituals link the Christian community to the past and propel the present community to build a common future together. It is through rituals that individuals bond into a community.[12]

Virtuous habits need to be practiced daily to be ingrained into our character. Michael Novak, Catholic religious writer, lists

---

7. Bellah et al., *Habits of the Heart*, xlviii.
8. Bellah et al., *Habits of the Heart*, 137.
9. Garber, *Fabric of Faithfulness*, 51.
10. Fletcher, *24/7 Christian*, 3.
11. Bellah et al., *Habits of the Heart*, 69.
12. Bellah et al., *Habits of the Heart*, 252, 282.

"four cardinal virtues: temperance, fortitude, practical wisdom, and justice."[13] I believe that the apostle Paul's fruit of the Spirit list encompasses the total realm of virtuous habits: love, joy, peace, patience, kindness, generosity, faithfulness, gentleness, and self-control (Gal 5:22–23). These nine virtues form the core of Christian character. One can quickly speak the words, but practicing the fruit of the Spirit daily is difficult without developing habits that constantly ingrain the fruit into our core character. When tempers flare or life gets difficult, the fruit of the Spirit can quickly dissipate without developing habits. And when a person fails, there is always God's grace to begin again.

Establishing habits moves theory into reality. Habits discipline and hone the mind, body, and spirit. *Charismata* develops and reaches its zenith. While God gives different gifts to individuals, all humans can benefit from habits.

FINAL COMMENTS

My mother taught elementary and middle school students in south Texas for many years before becoming an assistant principal. She loved children and enjoyed her work, except when she taught without air conditioning in the Texas summer heat. After she retired, she volunteered as a child advocate. She worked with state judges, lawyers, and families to determine the needs of abused or neglected children. Her role was to advocate for children within the Texas legal system. Judges praised her knowledge and expertise honed through years of teaching children. She was honored for her services by being named Advocate of the Year.

When I visited my parents after establishing a home of my own, I stayed in a guest room. On the top of a chest of drawers was a small sculpture with engraved words:

> A hundred years from now it will not matter what my bank account was, the sort of house I lived in, or the kind

---

13. Novak, *Business as a Calling*, 102.

of car I drove. But the world may be different because I was important in the life of a boy [child].

This quote is attributed to Forest Witcraft (1894–1967), a professional Scout trainer. It was published in an essay that begins: "I am not a Very Important Man."[14] Like my mother, Witcraft spent his life mentoring youths through their childhood years. Neither led lives of fame or wealth, athletic prowess or world championships, or political power on a world stage. Like almost all humans, their lives were ordinary lives shaped by their individual gifts within a community of family, friends, and faith. Their lives were significant, though. My mother shaped my life, which has cascaded down to my children and grandchildren. I joined Scouts at age eleven, and my scouting experiences transformed my life. Witcraft was a professional Scout leader who shaped the scouting program. His work cascaded down to me and my son.

Some believe that a significant life is a life that greatly influences many people, and a good life is simply having a moral character.[15] For me, a significant life begins with vocation, the comprehensive life of a Christian after positively responding to God's call to faith in Jesus Christ. It is faithful obedience to God by being part of God's mission of loving and serving one's neighbor with individual gifts. This is a good life, although suffering may happen along the journey.

One of my favorite movies is *It's a Wonderful Life*. I try to watch it every year during the Christmas season. It was released in 1946 to a war-weary nation and is considered one of the finest films ever produced. The leading character, George Bailey, played by Jimmy Stewart, wanted to leave his provincial life, and conquer the business world. Life throws obstacles in his path, and he is forced to make difficult choices. He reluctantly stays in his small town, marries, and raises a family while working in a small bank that provides affordable housing loans. When a crisis hits, George decides to kill himself because he believes he is worth more dead

---

14. Witcraft, "Within My Power."
15. Schwehn and Bass, *Leading Lives That Matter*, 8–9.

than alive. An angel, Clarence, saves him by showing him what others' lives would have been like if George had never lived. In one of the most famous movie scenes, George joyfully runs down the snowy main street yelling "Merry Christmas!" He reunites with his family hugging and kissing everyone. George realized he had a wonderful life.[16]

George was an ordinary man but led a life of significance. He worked for the common good and practiced Christian values. George lived a life of meaning, filled with loving family and friends. George thought that being significant was greatness measured by human standards; Christians recognize greatness as being a child of God. Vocation is the wholeness of life, responsibilities, and relationships. It is everything that brings humans into relationship with other humans. The question should not be why am I not significant like Martin Luther or President Obama, but how do I use my *charismata*? The journey of vocation begins with answering the call to faith, then it is a lifelong journey of developing your gifts, serving the common good, balancing choices, and establishing habits that reinforce your values. Vocation is not simply an occupation but a diversified portfolio of family, community, church, citizenship, leisure, and, yes, also work. Balancing this *charismata* portfolio is required for harmony and risk reduction.

The journey of vocation starts with knowing that, eventually, there will be an end to this earthly life. We are all mortal creatures; choose wisely and faithfully.

> He has told you, O mortal, what is good; and what does the Lord require of you but to do justice, and to love kindness, and to walk humbly with your God? (Mic 6:8)

---

16. Capra, *It's a Wonderful Life*.

Appendix
Glossary of Theological Terms

Calling—Hebrew: *qara'*, Greek: *klēsis*, Latin: *vocatio*, German: *Beruf*—Martin Luther's term for a Christian's earthly or spiritual work.[1] God's pursuit of individuals to a life of faith in Jesus Christ. The divine intervention is unique and personal to each person. Individuals freely decide whether to answer God's commands to love God and neighbors through service and stewardship. Positively answering God's call allows humans to find and fulfill their central purpose of life.[2] Synonymous with corporate, heavenly, holy,[3] general, ordinary, original, principal, special (Karl Barth),[4] spiritual, and universal callings. Related to the church (Greek: *ekklēsia*—"called ones"—and in classical Athens, it refers to a political assembly).

Career—*Carraria* (Latin for "a road for vehicles, a footpath, or path")[5] and *carriere* (Middle French for "a road or racecourse"). Professional life associated with an occupation that offers advancement and a variety of jobs. It is possible to have multiple careers in a lifetime. Synonymous with career path.

---

1. Wingren, *Luther on Vocation*, 1–2.
2. Guinness, *Call*, 7.
3. Schuurman, *Vocation*, 25–26.
4. Barth, *Doctrine of Creation*, 600.
5. Whelchel, *How Then*, 75.

Appendix

Charism—Greek: *charisma* (singular), *charismata* (plural). A spiritual gift. The Holy Spirit both calls and empowers with gifts to accomplish tasks. A theological term used by Miroslav Volf as the basis of his pneumatological understanding of work.[6]

Christology—The study of the person and work of Jesus Christ.

Community—Derived from *communis* (Latin, meaning "common") and *communicare* (Latin) meaning 'to give, receive, or participate.'

Cross of Vocation—Humans are to bear their own crosses for the sake of others in all difficulties. It alludes to the cross of Jesus Christ.[7]

Culture—The artificial and secondary environment that humans impose on nature. It includes language, habits, ideas, beliefs, customs, social organization, inherited artifacts, technical processes, and values. It is always social and involves human achievements, such as speech, education, tradition, myth, science, art, philosophy, government, law, rite, beliefs, inventions, and technologies. It centers on human values.[8]

Dialectic Theology—A theological movement, associated with Karl Barth and others, stressing the paradoxical nature of divine truths. For example, God is both grace and judgment.

Eschatology—The study of the "last things" or the end of the world, which includes the second coming of Jesus Christ and the last judgment.

Formal Call—A commission from a group of people.[9]

Grace—Greek: *charis*, Latin: *gratia*. Unmerited favor that is not deserved. Judgment that is deserved is withheld.[10]

---

6. Volf, *Work in the Spirit*, 113–14.
7. Wingren, *Luther on Vocation*, 29.
8. Niebuhr, *Christ and Culture*, 32–35.
9. Marshall, *Kind of Life*, 77.
10. McKim, *Westminster Dictionary of Theological Terms*, 120.

APPENDIX

Kingdom of God—God's sovereign reign and rule. It is a major focus of Jesus's teachings. Equivalent phrases are "kingdom of Jesus" and "kingdom of heaven."

Modern Period—Age of Enlightenment (1687–1900, the death of Friedrich Nietzsche). The beginning of philosophic reasoning and scientific discoveries that questioned religious doctrines and divine revelation. The focus is on reason and logic to determine truths.[11]

Moral Character—One's basic disposition or nature with regard to questions of right and wrong.

New Creation—The anticipated renewal of the created order by God in the "new heaven and new earth" as found in Rev 21:1; Rom 8:18–21; and 2 Pet 3:13.

Occupation—Work in which a person is employed, usually paid work. It has to do with current employment and a specific job description.[12] Synonymous with job, labor, and work. Antonym of leisure.

Orders—German: *Orden*. Martin Luther defines three God-given orders: (1) life in the home, (2) life in the state, (3) life in the church. These orders are for the sake of society, and all human activity happens within them.[13] Also, religious groups.

Parousia—An originally Greek term used for the "coming of Christ," most usually focused on the "second coming."

Particular Calling—A call to a specific occupation or service which unfolds over time and may change during a lifetime.[14] It is derived from the writings of the apostle Paul and references occupations only within the church: "And God has appointed in the church first apostles, second prophets, third teachers; then deeds of power,

---

11. Groothuis, *Truth Decay*, 33–37.
12. Whelchel, *How Then*, 75.
13. Bennethum, *Listen*, 51.
14. Denver Institute, *Study on Calling*, 4.

Appendix

then gifts of healing, forms of assistance, forms of leadership, various kinds of tongues. Are all apostles? Are all prophets? Are all teachers? Do all work miracles? Do all possess gifts of healing? Do all speak in tongues? Do all interpret?" (1 Cor 12:28–30). Synonymous with external (Martin Luther),[15] individual, secondary, special (John Calvin and Wuthnow),[16] and specific callings.[17]

Pneumatology—The theological study of the Holy Spirit.

Postmodern Period—After the modern period (post-1900). Rejected modernism as an invention of the dominant powers that was used as a political tool. Rationality is dismissed, and there are no objective truths. Moral values are constructed by cultures and religious traditions.[18]

Premodern Period—Prior to the age of Enlightenment (pre-1687, the publication of Isaac Newton's *Principia Mathematica*). Cultures had little to no diversity, minimal or no social change, no secularization, and were prescientific. Society was coherent with prescribed social roles.[19]

Profession—Latin: *professio*. The body of qualified persons of one specific occupation or field. Excellence is achieved through occupational achievements or obtaining higher levels of authority.

Protology—The study of the revealed doctrine of "first things," or the beginning of the world.

Righteous—Hebrew: *tsaddiq* (singular), *tsaddiqim* (plural). Individuals who are willing to disadvantage themselves for the common good of the community to advance God's justice and shalom, based on Prov 11:10: "When the righteous prosper, the city rejoices."[20]

15. Schuurman, *Vocation*, 17.
16. Placher, *Callings*, 232; Wuthnow, *Crisis in the Churches*, 22.
17. Schuurman, *Vocation*, 25–26.
18. Groothuis, *Truth Decay*, 38–40.
19. Groothuis, *Truth Decay*, 33–35.
20. Sherman, *Kingdom Calling*, 16–17.

Appendix

Sanctification—The process or result of God's continuing work in Christian believers through the power of the Holy Spirit.

Special Calling—God's specific, direct, and undeniable call to individuals to perform a task or mission. For example, Moses (Exod 3:1—4:17) and Saul (Acts 9:1–19). Synonymous with special mission.

Spiritual Gifts—Greek: *charisma* (singular), *charismata* (plural). Human talents that are sanctified by the Holy Spirit for service and the glory of God.[21] They are *both* the endowment and the call of God towards benefiting the common good[22] and accomplishing a particular task.[23]

Station—German: *Stand* (Martin Luther). Human roles during life, such as parent, child, worker, church member, state official, teacher, caregiver, etc., that humans are born into or choose during their lifetime. These roles are based on natural law, set by God's providence[24] for the care of human beings[25] and are linked to societal institutions.[26] Synonymous with duty, estate, occupation, office (German: *Amt*) and profession.

Sundry Callings—A subdivision of particular callings requiring special gifts, such as merchants and physicians.[27]

Talents—Human abilities endowed by God.[28]

Vocation—Latin: *vocare* (verb), *vocatio* (noun). The comprehensive life of a Christian after positively responding to God's call to faith in Jesus Christ. It is the wholeness of life, relationships, and

---

21. Stevens, *Doing God's Business*, 206; Wolters, *Creation Regained*, 105–6.
22. Volf, "Eschaton, Creation," 132.
23. Volf, *Work in the Spirit*, 114.
24. Badcock, *Way of Life*, 36–37.
25. Wingren, *Luther on Vocation*, 125.
26. Kolden, "Luther on Vocation," 382.
27. Marshall, *Kind of Life*, 43.
28. Stevens, *Doing God's Business*, 206.

responsibilities.[29] It is integral to God's mission,[30] the search for a basis for human identity, and the understanding of humanness itself.[31] It is everything that brings humans into relationships with other humans.[32] It is faithful obedience to God[33] and being set apart for God's purpose[34] to love and serve one's neighbor.[35] It is human life in the Holy Spirit,[36] with each believer bearing the fruit of the Spirit.[37]

Vocational Power—Leveraging human knowledge/expertise, platforms, networks, position, influence, skills, and reputation/fame.[38]

Vocational Stewardship—The intentional and strategic deployment of vocational power towards the kingdom of God.[39]

Weighty Callings—A subdivision of particular callings that are more general, such as family, church, and commonwealth.[40]

---

29. Garber, *Visions of Vocation*, 11.
30. Garber, *Visions of Vocation*, 18.
31. Guinness, *Call*, 20.
32. Hardy, *Fabric of Faithfulness*, 111–12.
33. Marshall, *Kind of Life*, 24.
34. Denver Institute, *Study on Calling*, 3.
35. Veith, *God at Work*, 39–40.
36. Badcock, *Way of Life*, 123.
37. Schuurman, *Vocation*, 26.
38. Sherman, *Kingdom Calling*, 16–17, 121.
39. Sherman, *Kingdom Calling*, 20.
40. Marshall, *Kind of Life*, 43.

Bibliography

Albion, Mark. *Making a Life, Making a Living.* New York: Warner, 2000.
Albom, Mitch. *Tuesdays with Morrie: An Old Man, a Young Man, and Life's Greatest Lesson.* New York: Broadway, 2017.
Alexander, Neil M., ed. *The Book of Discipline of The United Methodist Church: 2012.* Nashville: United Methodist, 2012.
Badcock, Gary D. *The Way of Life: A Theology of Christian Vocation.* Grand Rapids: Eerdmans, 1998.
Banks, Robert, and R. Paul Stevens, eds. *The Complete Book of Everyday Christianity: An A-to-Z Guide to Following Christ in Every Aspect of Life.* Downers Grove, IL: InterVarsity, 1997.
Barnes, Kenneth J. *Redeeming Capitalism.* Grand Rapids: Eerdmans, 2018.
Barth, Karl. *The Doctrine of Creation.* Vol. 3, pt. 4 of *Church Dogmatics.* Edinburgh: T&T Clark, 1961.
Bellah, Robert N., et al. *Habits of the Heart.* Berkeley: University of California Press, 2008.
Bennethum, D. Michael. *Listen! God Is Calling! Luther Speaks of Vocation, Faith, and Work.* Minneapolis: Augsburg Fortress, 2003.
Bernbaum, John A., and Simon M. Steer. *Why Work? Careers and Employment in Biblical Perspective.* Grand Rapids: Baker, 1986.
Bonhoeffer, Dietrich. *The Cost of Discipleship.* Translated by R. H. Fuller, with some revision by Irmgard Booth. New York: Touchstone, 1995.
Brooks, David. *The Second Mountain: The Quest for a Moral Life.* New York: Random House, 2019.
Brunner, Emil. *Christianity and Civilisation.* New York: Charles Scribner's Sons, 1949.
Buechner, Frederick. *Wishful Thinking: A Theological ABC.* New York: HarperSanFrancisco, 1973.
Calvin, John. *Commentary on a Harmony of the Evangelists, Matthew, Mark, and Luke.* Translated by William Pringle. John Calvin Bible Commentaries 2. Grand Rapids: Eerdmans, 1949.
———. *Commentary on the Epistles of Paul the Apostle to the Corinthians.* Translated by John Pringle. Calvin Commentaries 1. Grand Rapids: Eerdmans, 1948.

Bibliography

———. *The First Epistle of Paul the Apostle to the Corinthians*. Translated by John W. Fraser. Calvin's Commentaries. Grand Rapids: Eerdmans, 1960.

———. *Institutes of the Christian Religion*. Translated by Henry Beveridge. Peabody, MA: Hendrickson, 2008.

Capra, Frank, dir. *It's a Wonderful Life*. New York: RKO, 1946.

Christian History. "Gifts That Differ; Callings That Unite: An Interview with Will Messenger." *Christian History* 110 (2014) 4–6.

Claar, Victor V., and Robin J. Klay. *Economics in Christian Perspective: Theory, Policy and Life Choices*. Downers Grove, IL: IVP Academic, 2007.

Conyers, A. J. "The Meaning of Vocation." In *Vocation*, edited by Robert B. Kruschwitz, 11–19. Christian Reflection: A Series in Faith and Ethics. Waco: The Center for Christian Ethics at Baylor University, 2004. https://ifl.web.baylor.edu/sites/g/files/ecbvkj771/files/2023-02/vocation.pdf.

Covey, Stephen R. *The 7 Habits of Highly Effective People: Powerful Lessons in Personal Change*. New York: Simon & Schuster, 2013.

Crouch, Andy. *Culture Making: Recovering Our Creative Calling*. Downers Grove, IL: IVP, 2008.

Denver Institute for Faith and Work. *A Study on Calling: New Thoughts for an Old Idea*. Centennial, CO: Denver Institute for Faith and Work, 2023. https://denverinstitute.org/a-study-on-calling/.

Doriani, Daniel M. *Work: Its Purpose, Dignity, and Transformation*. Phillipsburg, NJ: P&R, 2019.

Douglas, Richard M. "Talent and Vocation in Humanist and Protestant Thought." In *Action and Conviction in Early Modern Europe: Essays in Memory of E. H. Harbison*, edited by Theodore K. Rabb and Jerrold E. Seigel, 261–98. Princeton Legacy Library. Reprint, Princeton, NJ: Princeton University Press, 2015.

Ellul, Jacques. "Work and Calling." *Katallagete* 4 (1972) 8–16. https://www.yumpu.com/en/document/view/35121449/jacques-ellul-jesus-radicals.

Fee, Gordon D., ed. *The First Epistle to the Corinthians*. Rev. ed. New International Commentary on the New Testament. Grand Rapids: Eerdmans, 2014.

Fink, David C. "Liberating Those Who Work: Martin Luther Challenged Centuries of Vocational Reflection." *Christian History* 110 (2014) 20–22.

Fletcher, Christine M. *24/7 Christian: The Secular Vocation of the Laity*. Collegeville, MN: Liturgical, 2015.

Frankl, Viktor E. *Man's Search for Meaning*. Boston: Beacon, 2006.

Garber, Steven. *The Fabric of Faithfulness: Weaving Together Belief and Behavior*. Expanded ed. Downers Grove, IL: InterVarsity, 2007.

———. *Visions of Vocation: Common Grace for the Common Good*. Downers Grove, IL: InterVarsity, 2014.

Gill, David W. "Jacques Ellul on Vocation & the Ethics of the Workplace." *Radix Magazine* 22 (1994) 10–13, 28–29. https://robertoigarza.files.wordpress.com/2011/02/ent-jacques-ellul-on-vocation-ethics-of-the-workplace-gill-1994.pdf.

BIBLIOGRAPHY

González, Justo L. *The Story of Christianity*. 3 vols. New York: HarperCollins, 2010.

Groothuis, Douglas. *Truth Decay: Defending Christianity against the Challenges of Postmodernism*. Updated anniv. ed. Downers Grove, IL: InterVarsity, 2000.

Guinness, Os. *The Call: Finding and Fulfilling the Central Purpose of Your Life*. Nashville: W, 2003.

Hardy, Lee. *The Fabric of This World: Inquiries into Calling, Career Choice, and the Design of Human Work*. Grand Rapids: Eerdmans, 1990.

Heiges, Donald R. *The Christian's Calling*. Philadelphia: Muhlenberg, 1958.

Hendricks, Bill. *The Person Called You: Why You're Here, Why You Matter & What You Should Do with Your Life*. Chicago: Moody, 2014.

Higginson, Richard. *Questions of Business Life: Exploring Workplace Issues from a Christian Perspective*. Carlisle, UK: Spring Harvest, 2002.

Holl, Karl. "The History of the Word *Vocation* (*Beruf*)." Translated by Heber F. Peacock. *Review and Exposition* 55 (1958) 126–54.

Kee, Howard C., and Montgomery J. Shroyer. *The Bible and God's Call: A Study of the Biblical Foundation of Vocation*. Nashville: Cokesbury, 1962.

Keller, Timothy. "Creation Care and Justice." Sermon at Redeemer Presbyterian Church, New York, Jan. 16, 2005. https://podcast.gospelinlife.com/e/creation-care-and-justice-1637090616/.

Kolden, Marc. "Luther on Vocation." *Word & World* 3/4 (1983) 382–90. https://wordandworld.luthersem.edu/content/pdfs/3-4_Luther/3-4_Kolden.pdf.

Luther, Martin. *Church and Ministry 2*. Vol. 40 of *Luther's Works*. Edited by Conrad Bergendoff and Helmut T. Lehmann. Philadelphia: Fortress, 1958.

———. *Commentaries on 1 Corinthians 7, 1 Corinthians 15; Lectures on 1 Timothy*. Vol. 28 of *Luther's Works*. Edited by Hilton C. Oswald. St. Louis: Concordia, 1973.

———. *Lectures on Galatians 1535: Chapters 5–6; Lectures on Galatians 1519: Chapters 1–6*. Vol. 27 of *Luther's Works*. Edited by Jaroslav Pelikan. St. Louis: Concordia, 1964.

———. *Lectures on Genesis: Chapters 15–20*. Vol. 3 of *Luther's Works*. Edited by Jaroslav Pelikan. St. Louis: Concordia, 1961.

———. *Lectures on Romans*. Vol. 25 of *Luther's Works*. Edited by Hilton C. Oswald. St. Louis: Concordia, 1972.

———. *Selected Psalms 2*. Vol. 13 of *Luther's Works*. Edited by Jaroslav Pelikan. St. Louis: Concordia, 1956.

———. *The Sermon on the Mount (Sermons) and The Magnificat*. Vol. 21 of *Luther's Works*. Edited by Jaroslav Pelikan. St. Louis: Concordia, 1956.

———. *Sermons on the Gospel of St. John: Chapters 6–8*. Vol. 23 of *Luther's Works*. Edited by Jaroslav Pelikan and Daniel E. Poellot. St. Louis: Concordia, 1959.

Mackenzie, Alistair, and Wayne Kirkland. *Where's God on Monday? Integrating Faith and Work Every Day of the Week*. Colorado Springs, CO: Nav, 2003.

BIBLIOGRAPHY

Mackenzie, Alistair., et al. *Soul Purpose: Making a Difference in Life and Work.* Christchurch, NZ: Nav, 2004.

Marshall, Paul. *A Kind of Life Imposed on Man: Vocation and Social Order from Tyndale to Locke.* Heritage. Toronto: University of Toronto Press, 1996.

Marshall, Paul., et al. *Labour of Love: Essays on Work.* Toronto: Wedge, 1980.

Maslow, A. H. "A Theory of Human Motivation." *Psychological Review* 50 (1943) 370–96.

Martin, James. *Between Heaven and Mirth: Why Joy, Humor, and Laughter Are at the Heart of the Spiritual Life.* New York: HarperCollins, 2011.

McGrath, Alister. "Calvin and the Christian Calling." *First Things* 94 (1999) 31–35. https://www.firstthings.com/article/1999/06/calvin-and-the-christian-calling.

McKim, Donald K. *Westminster Dictionary of Theological Terms.* Louisville: Westminster John Knox, 1996.

Nelson, John Oliver, ed. *Work and Vocation: A Christian Discussion.* New York: Harper & Brothers, 1954.

Nelson, Tom. *Work Matters: Connecting Sunday Worship to Monday Work.* Wheaton, IL: Crossway, 2011.

Neuser, W. H. "The First Outline of Calvin's Theology—The Preface to the New Testament in the Olivétan Bible of 1535." *Koers* 66 (2001) 1–39.

Niebuhr, H. Richard. *Christ and Culture.* New York: HarperOne, 2001.

Novak, Michael. *Business as a Calling: Work and the Examined Life.* New York: Free, 1996.

Palmer, Parker J. *Let Your Life Speak: Listening for the Voice of Vocation.* San Francisco: Jossey-Bass, 2000.

Perkins, William. "A Treatise of the Vocations, or Callings of Men, with the Sorts and Kinds of Them, and the Right Use of Them." Monergism, Jan. 2015. Edited by William H. Gross. https://www.monergism.com/treatise-vocations-ebook.

Placher, William C., ed. *Callings: Twenty Centuries of Christian Wisdom on Vocation.* Grand Rapids: Eerdmans, 2005.

Richardson, Alan. *The Biblical Doctrine of Work.* London: SCM, 1963.

Schuster, John P. *Answering Your Call: A Guide for Living Your Deepest Purpose.* San Francisco: Berrett-Koehler, 2003.

Schuurman, Douglas J. "Creation, Eschaton, and Social Ethics: A Response to Volf." *Calvin Theological Journal* 30 (1995) 144–58.

———. *Vocation: Discerning Our Callings in Life.* Grand Rapids: Eerdmans, 2004.

Schwehn, Mark. R., and Dorothy C. Bass, eds. *Leading Lives That Matter: What We Should Do and Who We Should Be.* Grand Rapids: Eerdmans, 2006.

Sherman, Amy L. *Kingdom Calling: Vocational Stewardship for the Common Good.* Downers Grove, IL: IVP, 2011.

Stevens, R. Paul. *Doing God's Business: Meaning and Motivation for the Marketplace.* Grand Rapids: Eerdmans, 2006.

BIBLIOGRAPHY

Troeltsch, Ernst. *The Social Teaching of the Christian Churches.* Translated by Olive Wyon. 2 vols. Louisville: Westminster John Knox, 1992.

Veith, Gene Edward, Jr. *God at Work: Your Christian Vocation in All of Life.* Wheaton, IL: Crossway, 2002.

———. "Vocation Is in the Here and Now: Four Christian Thinkers Reflect on How God Called Them and Calls Us." *Christian History* 110 (2014) 42–45.

Volf, Miroslav. "Eschaton, Creation, and Social Ethics." *Calvin Theological Journal* 30 (1995) 130–43.

———. *Work in the Spirit: Toward a Theology of Work.* Reprint, Eugene, OR: Wipf and Stock, 2001.

Walton, John H. *Ancient Near Eastern Thought and the Old Testament: Introducing the Conceptual World of the Hebrew Bible.* 2nd ed. Grand Rapids: Baker Academic, 2018.

———. *The Lost World of Genesis One.* Vol. 2 of *Ancient Cosmology and the Origins Debate.* Lost World. Downers Grove, IL: IVP Academic, 2009.

Weber, Max. *The Protestant Ethic and the Spirit of Capitalism.* Translated by Stephen Kalberg. Rev. 1920 ed. New York: Oxford University Press, 2011.

Whelchel, Hugh. *How Then Should We Work: Rediscovering the Biblical Doctrine of Work.* McLean, VA: Institute for Faith, Work & Economics, 2012.

Wingren, Gustaf. *Luther on Vocation.* Translated by Carl C. Rasmussen. Eugene, OR: Wipf and Stock, 2004.

Winslade, William J. "Afterword." In *Man's Search for Meaning*, by Viktor E. Frankl, 155–65. Boston: Beacon, 2006.

Witcraft, Forest E. "Within My Power." *Scouting* 38 (1950) 2.

Witherington, Ben, III. *Work: A Kingdom Perspective on Labor.* Grand Rapids: Eerdmans, 2011.

Wolters, Albert M. *Creation Regained: Biblical Basics for a Reformational Worldview.* Grand Rapids: Eerdmans, 1985.

Wong, Kenman L., and Scott B. Rae. *Business for the Common Good: A Christian Vision for the Marketplace.* Christian Worldview Integration. Downers Grove, IL: IVP Academic, 2011.

Wuthnow, Robert. *The Crisis in the Churches: Spiritual Malaise, Fiscal Woe.* New York: Oxford University Press, 1997.

Subject Index

Aaron, 5, 6, 7, 13
abilities, God's endowment of, 8, 9. *See also* gifts/giftings; talents
Abraham, 5, 10
Age of Enlightenment, xvii, 45, 53, 72, 113
Ahab, 5
American Revolutionary War, 53
angelic choirs, 29
Anglicans, 45
Anthony, Saint, 25, 27
Aquinas, Thomas, 29
asceticism, 51
ascriptivism, 68
athletic giftings, 78, 97, 99–100
authorities/officials, 67, 88
Azariah, 9

Badcock, Gary D., 69–73, 89–90
baptism, 34
Barmen Declaration, 56
Barnabas, 11
Barth, Karl, 56–60, 61, 79, 93, 111, 112
Baxter, Richard, 46–47, 48, 51, 83
Beacon, Thomas, 45–46
benevolence, 7, 14
Berlin, 86
Berthold of Regensburg, Saint, 29
Beruf, 33–34, 36–37, 65
Bezalel, 6
Bible of Olivétan, 43

Biel, Gabriel, 30
Bonhoeffer, Dietrich, 23, 86, 93
Bonn University, 56
Bordeaux University, 60
Buechner, Frederick, 81

calling
  choosing, 48
  defined, 111
  determination of, 69
  faith and, 13, 67
  general, 43, 47, 64
  as gift, 21
  of God, 4, 5–7, 10, 57–58, 61, 111
  as natural right, 50
  openness to change in, 60
  personal, 47–48
  sanctification and, 23
  special, 43–44, 115
  to tasks, 13
  vocation and, 71
Calvin College, 66
Calvin, John, 39–45, 47, 66, 88, 114
Calvinism, xvii, 44–45, 51, 53
Cambridge University, 30
capitalism, xvii, 28, 53–55, 62
career, defined, 111. *See also* vocation
Cassian, John, Saint, 27
celibacy, 16, 20, 23

Subject Index

character, habits of the heart and, 105–106
charism, 112
Charles I (king), 49
Charles II (king), 49
Charles V (Roman emperor), 32
Charles University, 31
Charnock, Stephen, 50
China, 92
choices/choosing
   of culture, 92–95
   factors regarding, 89–90
   by God, 5, 10
   by Jesus Christ, 12
   of leisure, 99–100
   of location, 97–99
   of money, 95–96
   of moral life, 90–91
   overview of, 89–90
   of success, 96–97
Christians/Christianity
   bureaucracy of, 26
   characteristics of, 71
   cultural struggle against, 25, 92, 93–94
   moral boundaries of, 91
   persecution of, 25
   quality of life characteristics of, 65–66
   radical, 27
   relationship with God and, 23
   ritual habits of, 106
   sexual immorality of, 20
   social status and, 20–21
Christology, 112
church
   bureaucracy of, 26
   persecution and, 25
   segregation in, 27
   spiritual gifts in, 17, 18
   state and, 28
   vocational hierarchy in, 27, 32–33
Church of England, 44, 45
circumcision, 21–22

citizenship, in community, 85–86
civic service, 85–86
clearness committee, 83
commanding, by God, 10
common good, 87–89
community, 84–89, 103–104, 106, 112
Constantine the Great, 25
Council of Constance, 31
Covey, Stephen, 105
craftsmen, 6, 8
creation story, 4
crisis theology, 56
cross of vocation, 35, 42, 68, 112
Crouch, Andy, 94
Crowley, Robert, 45
culture, 25, 92–95, 112
Cyrus II (king), 5–6

Daniel, 9
David, 5
Descartes, René, 50
dialectical theology, 56, 112
disciples, 11–12
divorce, 20, 23
donation, of gifts, 14–15
Dunn, Stephen, xiii

Eckhart, Meister, 29
economic traditionalism, 28
Edict of Milan, 25
Edinburgh University, 69
education, 55
Eisenach, 32
Eisleben, 31
Eli, 5
Elijah, 12–13
Elizabethan Age, 45
Elizabeth I (queen), 49
Ellul, Jacques, 60–63
energy industry, xiv
English Civil War, 49
English Reformation, 45
Enlightenment, xvii, 45, 53, 72, 113

Subject Index

entertainment, cultural choices regarding, 94
equal rights, 27
Erfurt, 31
eschatology, 64–65, 112
Eusebius of Caesarea, 27

faith, xv–xvi, 13, 41, 67
faithfulness, in vocation, 81–82
fall of man, 43
Fee, Gordon D., 19–20
flat people, 102
formal call, 112. *See also* calling
Forster, E. M., 102
Frankl, Viktor, 85, 93
Franklin, Benjamin, 53–54
Frederick III (Prince), 32
Freiburg University, 40
freedom, 22

general calling, 43, 47, 64
Geneva, 39
gentiles, 14
giftedness, defined, 78
gifts/giftings. *See also* spiritual gifts
  benevolence and, 14
  for common good, 68
  community for, 84–89
  contentedness with, 43
  as contributing to public good, 85, 87–89
  development of, 66, 79–80
  diversity of, 78
  donation and, 14–15
  God's use of, 57–58
  guidance and, 82–84
  Holy Spirit's role regarding, 14, 17, 35, 38, 41–42, 43, 112
  Miroslav Volf's idea of, 66
  in the New Testament, 14–19
  in the Old Testament, 7–8
  passion for, 81–82
  self-actualization and, 78–81
  as service to neighbors, 80
  specialization, 78–79
  supply and demand of, 80–81
  as talent, 15–19

God
  action of, 3
  benevolence of, 7
  call of, 4, 5–7, 10, 57–58, 61, 111
  choosing by, 5, 10
  commanding by, 10
  glorification of, 40
  invitation by, 5, 10
  king-making by, 5
  love of, 97
  naming by, 4, 10
  proclamations of, 4
  providence of, 69
  revelation of, 57, 61
  separating by, 5
  shouting by, 4
  summons of, 4, 10–11, 57

Good Will Hunting (film), 98
Goodwin, John, 49–50
good works, 41
grace, 14, 18–19, 112
grasshopper/ant analogy, 84
Greco-Roman slaves, 22
greed, 28
guidance, in giftings, 82–84
Gutenberg, Johannes, 31–32

habits, establishing, 104–107
Hananiah, 9
Hardy, Lee, 66
Havel, Vaclav, 87
Heidelburg University, 40
Hendricks, Bill, 78
Henry VIII (king), 44
hierarchy, vocational, 27, 32–33, 37
Hiram of Tyre, 8
Hitler, Adolf, 56, 86
holiness, 13, 67
Holy Spirit, 14, 17, 35, 38, 41, 43, 112

Subject Index

Hooper, John, 46
human reasoning, relying on, 83
Huron University, 69
Hus, Jan, 31

idleness, 46–47, 51
image of God, 16
incarnation, vocational, 62, 63
individualism, 85, 105–106
industrial age, 55
intelligence, gifting of, 8
interdependence, 103
investing, 101–102
investment portfolio theory, 101–102
invitation, by God, 5, 10
Israelites, 5, 7
It's a Wonderful Life (film), 108–109

James, 12
James VI of Scotland (James I of England), 49
Jehu, 5
Jerome, Saint, 25–26
Jesus Christ, 10, 11–13, 14–15, 80, 89, 92
John, 12
joy, from work, 63

Keller, Timothy, 88–89
King, Martin Luther, Jr., 65
kingdom of God, 113
king-making, by God, 5

Lazarus, 12
laziness, 46–47, 51, 80
leisure, 99–100
Levi, tribe of, 5, 6–7, 13
location, choices of, 97–99
London, 92, 98
love of God, 97
Luther, Martin, 30–39, 49, 63, 68, 70, 71, 111, 113, 114

Mainz, 31
marriage, 16, 20–21, 23
Marshall, Paul, 45
Martha, 29
Marx, Karl, 61–62, 64
Mary, 12, 29
Mary (mother of Jesus), 15
mediators, role of, 6
Middle Ages, 54–55
Mishael, 9
model of work, self-actualization in, 77–84
Modern Period-Age of Enlightenment, xvii, 113
Moltmann, Jürgen, 64
monasticism, 24–30
money, 28, 47, 95–96
Moorman, Rebecca, x, xvii
moral character, 91, 108, 113
moral life, choices regarding, 90–91
mortality, 108
Moses, 5, 6, 83

naming, by God and Jesus, 4, 10, 12
Nazis, 56, 60, 86, 93
Nebuchadnezzar II (king), 7
neo-orthodox theology, 56
new creation, 113
New Testament, vocation in, 9–19
Newton, Isaac, xvi, 114
Niebuhr, H. Richard, 27, 93
Nietzsche, Friedrich, xvii, 113
Ninety-Five Theses (Luther), 32
Novak, Michael, 106–107

occupation, defined, 113. *See also* vocation
officials/authorities, 67, 88
Old Testament, vocation in, 3–9
orders, defined, 113
Orléans University, 39
Oxford University, 30–31

Subject Index

paganism, 26
Palmer, Parker, 78, 82–83
parable of the talents, 44, 80
Paris University, 30
parousia, 113
particular calling, 113–114. *See also* calling
passion, 81–82
pastors, 35–36
Paul, 14, 15–24, 87, 107
Perkins, William, 46, 48, 83
persecution, 25
personal calling, 47–48. *See also* calling
Peter, 19
Philip, 15
pneumatology, 114
Poole, Matthew, 50
Postmodern Period, xvii, 72, 56–72, 114
predestination, 40, 79
Premodern Period, xvi, 3–52, 114
priests, 6–7, 8, 26–27, 30, 33, 35–36
printing press, 31–32
proclamations, of God, 4
profession, defined, 114. *See also* vocation
Protestantism, 53
Protestant Reformation, 51
protology, 114
Provincetown Harbour (Cape Cod), 52
Pruett, Robert Jesse, ix, xvi–xvii
Puritans, 45–52, 71–72, 88

racial injustice, 22
radical Christianity, 27
reasoning, 50
Redeemer Presbyterian Church, New York City, 88
remarriage, 20
responsibility, 86–87
righteous, defined, 114
rituals, 106

rounded (portfolio) people, 102
The Rule of St. Benedict, 27

Sabbath, 50, 80
Salamanca University, 30
salvation, 41
sanctification, 23, 115
Sarai/Sarah, 4
Saul, 5, 6, 11
saying, by Jesus, 12
Schuurman, Douglas J., 66, 67–69
Second Great Awakening, 55
segregation, 27
self-actualization, 77–84
separating, by God, 5
serving, 18–19
sexual relations, 16, 20
shouting, 4, 12
singleness, 22–23
skills, God's command regarding, 7–9
slavery, 22
social media, 95
social movement, 37, 42
social order, angelic choirs of, 29
social status, 21
Solomon, 5, 7, 8
speaking, 18–19
speaking in tongues, 16
special calling, 43–44, 115. *See also* calling
specialization, of gifts, 78–79
sphere of operation, 58, 60
spiritual gifts, 15–18, 87–88, 115. *See also* gifts/giftings
spiritual perfection, 30
state, church and, 28
station, 33, 37, 38–39, 43, 115
St. Olaf College, 67
Strasbourg, 39
Stewart, Jimmy, 107–108
success, choices regarding, 96–97
summons/summoning, 4, 10–11, 12–13, 57

Subject Index

sundry callings, 115. *See also* calling

Taiwan, 92
talents, 15, 19, 44, 115. *See also* gifts/giftings
Tauler, Johannes, 30
technology, remote work and, 98–99
Tertullian, 26
Third Great Awakening, 55
Thomas Aquinas, 29
time, 23, 47
Timothy, 18
Tocqueville, Alexis de, 105–106
A Treatise of the Vocations (Perkins), 46
tsaddiqim, 88–89, 114
Tübingen University, 64
Tyndale, William, 45

Union Theological Seminary, 86
United Methodist Church, 92, 95
University of Bologna, 30

virtues, 106–107
vocation
  calling and, 71
  changes in, 60
  Charismata portfolio of, 101–109
  choosing, 48
  considerations regarding, 58–59
  cross of, 35, 42, 68, 112
  cultural interpretation of, xvi
  defined, xvi, 72, 115–116
  as to do the will of God, 70
  as employed for common good, 87–89
  faithfulness in, 81–82
  faith integration into, xv–xvi
  following age of Enlightenment, 72
  freedom of, 68
  as glorifying God, 19, 40
  as governed by God's will, 67
  hierarchy of, 27
  as individual redemption, 61
  journey of, xvi–xviii
  limitations of, 57
  mastery of, 79
  in the New Testament, 9–19
  in the Old Testament, 3–9
  as personal, 13–14
  purpose of, 34–35
  Reformational concept of, 67
  as religious occupations, 26–27
  responsibility in, 86–87
  seeking counsel regarding, 82–83
  as service to neighbors, 32–33
  themes of, 67
  as whole life, 21
vocational power, 116
vocational stewardship, 116
vocation theology
  of Douglas J. Schuurman, 67–69
  of Gary D. Badcock, 69–73, 89–90
  of Jacques Ellul, 60–63
  of John Calvin, 39, 40–45, 66, 88
  of Karl Barth, 56–60, 61, 79
  of Martin Luther, 32–39, 49, 63, 65, 66, 70, 71
  of Miroslav Volf, 64–66, 68, 112
  secular definitions of, 49
Volf, Miroslav, 64–66, 68, 112
volunteer work, 62
von Harnack, Adolf, 56
the Vulgate, 25–26, 30–31

Waldo, Peter, 31
Wartburg Castle, 32
Watson, Thomas, 49
wealth creation, 47
Weber, Max, 40, 41, 46, 51

Subject Index

weighty callings, 116. *See also* calling
Wesley, John, 94–95
White, David, ix
will of God, 58, 70
wise men, 14–15
Witcraft, Forest, 107–108
Wittenberg University, 31
work, 28, 62–63. *See also* vocation

Work in the Spirit (Volf), 64, 68
World Athletic Championship (WAC), 78
worship, ritual habits of, 106
Wuthnow, Robert, 114
Wycliffe, John, 31

Yale University, 64

Scripture Index

OLD TESTAMENT

Genesis

1:5	4
1:10	3
17:10–14	21
17:15	4
22:14	3

Exodus

3:1—4:17	83, 115
3:4	6
19:6	7
19:20	4
26:1	7
26:31	7
28	8
28:3	8
28:6	7
28:15	7
31:1–11	6, 8
31:3	8
31:6	8
35:30—36:2	6
35:30—36:7	8
35:31	8
35:35	8, 9
36:1–2	8
36:8	7
36:35	7
39:3	7
39:8	7

Leviticus

7:35–36	6

Numbers

3:5–10	6
8:5–22	6
16:1–11	7
16:5	6
16:7	6
16:9	5, 7
18:6	7
18:7	7
18:19	7
19:7	7

Deuteronomy

5:12	106
10:8	5
18:5	5, 7
21:5	7
33:13	7
33:16	7

1 Samuel

3:4	4

Scripture Index

(1 Samuel continued)

15:11	5
15:17	6
15:35	5
16:8–10	5

1 Kings

3:7	5
7:14	8
8:16	5

2 Kings

9:3	5
9:6	5
9:12	5

1 Chronicles

15:2	5, 7
23:13	5, 6
28:4	5

2 Chronicles

1:8	5
1:9	5
1:11	5
22:7	5
29:11	7

Psalms

51:17	36
68:28	4
105:26	6

Proverbs

2:6	8
11:10	114

Isaiah

41:2	6
41:25	6
43:1	4
45:1	6
45:3	6
45:4	5, 6
46:11	6
48:12	5
48:15	6
51:2	5
56:7	10

Jeremiah

50:29	4
51:27	4

Daniel

1:17	9

Amos

5:8	4
7:4	4

Micah

6:8	71, 109

Haggai

1:11	4

Zechariah

3:10	5

Scripture Index

NEW TESTAMENT

Matthew	
2:11	14–15
5:9	12
6:24	95
10:1	11
21:13	10
22:17–21	95
25:14–30	44, 58, 80
25:15	44
25:31–46	80
25:46	80
28:18–20	103

Mark	
1:16–20	23
2:27	50
10:18	12

Luke	
6:13	11, 12
8:8	12
10:38–42	29
18:19	12

John	
1:42	12
8:12	34

Acts	
6:1–7	92
9:1–19	115
10:45	14
13:2	11
16:10	10
21:9	15

Romans	
1:1	11
1:6	10
1:7	10
1:11	14
8:18–21	113
8:28	11
8:29	11
8:30	10
12:3–8	15
12:6	15
12:6–8	15

1 Corinthians	
1:1	11
1:1–3	16
1:2	10
1:5	16
1:7	16
1:9	11, 20–21
1:26	14
3:1—4:21	16
4:7	16
7:1–7	20
7:1–16	20, 21
7:1–40	16
7:5	16
7:7	16
7:8–9	20
7:9	23
7:10–11	20
7:12–16	20
7:15	11, 20, 23
7:17	11, 21, 23
7:17–24	19–20, 24, 68, 70, 71
7:18–19	21
7:19	21
7:20	22, 23, 29, 36–37, 38, 50, 59, 65, 68
7:21	22
7:21–23	22
7:22	10
7:23	22
7:24	23

Scripture Index

(1 Corinthians continued)

7:25–40	20
7:29–31	23
10:31	11
12	15, 16, 58
12:1	17, 18
12:4	17
12:5–6	38–39
12:8–11	17
12–14	15, 87–88
12:14–26	17
12:27	17
12:27–31	17
12:28	17
12:28–30	114
12:30	17
12:31	17
13	15
14	15, 16, 17
14:1	18
14:12	18
28–31	64

2 Corinthians

9:5	15

Galatians

1:15	11
3:15	10
5:13	10
5:22–23	107
5:22–26	95
6:4	37

Ephesians

1:18	9, 11
3:7	14
4:4	11
4:8	18
4:11	18
4:12	18

Philippians

3:4	10

Colossians

3:15	11

1 Thessalonians

4:7	10

2 Thessalonians

2:14	9, 10

1 Timothy

4:1—5:2	18
4:13	18
4:14	18
6:6–10	95
6:12	10

2 Timothy

1:6	18

Hebrews

9:15	10
11:8	10

1 Peter

1:15	13
2:9	10, 32
4:10	18–19

2 Peter

3:13	113

Jude

1:1	10

Scripture Index

Revelation

17:14	11
19:9	10
21:1	113
21:6	14

www.ingramcontent.com/pod-product-compliance
Lightning Source LLC
Chambersburg PA
CBHW060824190426
43197CB00038B/2260